TRAVELING WITH ANGELS

Yolanda Montalvo

EXPRESSO
331 Newman Springs Road,
Red Bank, New Jersey, 07701
1-888-251-6088 ext 101
info@expressopublishing.com

TABLE OF CONTENTS

THE BATTLE

"They're coming!" David shouted. "I know"

The enemy was only a couple of miles away. As they were getting closer, God's Angels came down in a split second and intercepted them. God's Angels are beautiful angelic beings. . They are about the height of ten feet tall and wear a gold and silver plate covering their chest, over their white robe that is to their ankles, with a gold belt around their waist to signify their God's Warriors.

The enemy is at a distance, and they're coming in the thousands. They are flying towards me. I see God's Angels fighting the Demons. Demons are hideous creatures, dark evil looking serpents. They want to take mankind's souls to destroy them. And now they were after me. I was caught up in a battle and standing alongside God's Angels. I know I was too deep in the spirit world. It was not my intention to be in their world this long.

It was late in the evening, but not dark. I could hear the battle near my apartment. The fighting was closer than I thought. I think they are right above my apartment, it is hard to tell. They are fighting above about a couple a thousand feet. I could see more of them coming, from the north west of town. The enemy is getting closer, like a swarm of bees coming in the thousands flying toward us. I saw God's Angels fly down to intercept the Demons. Some of the Demons must have been nearby. Possibly hiding somewhere in the area.

There fighting in the sky, swords clanging, Angels and Demons fighting. I ask God for the Holy Spirit to come down and cover my apartment. The enemy cannot cross the Holy Spirit, much less get close to it. If they try to get near it, they immediately die. Dying for the enemy was to be sent back to Sheol. Sheol is a fiery pit of Hell. Where evil souls are tormented day and night for their sins.

I did not know if God was going to allow me to ask for the Holy Spirit but I asked anyway. The Holy Spirit is very powerful. The clanging of Swords was getting louder and louder. And from a distance away God's mighty Angels Warrior thrust their swords at the enemy.

I was getting tired of concentrating lying here on top of my bed with my eyes closed. It seemed as though the battle was going on forever. I am not afraid, I can not be afraid. If I fear them, then where is my faith? Must be strong, God is with me. That is what I believe. That is what I kept telling myself, trying not to think about it too much. I never felt I wanted to cry, the whole time this was going on. I had no fear, I do not know why? I was getting tired and sleepy.

"Boddie wake up, wake up Boddie, do not fall asleep," David shouted.

I was just so sleepy. I knew if I fell asleep now, it was possible for them to kill me. Must stay awake. I have to close my eyes to see what is going on, in my vision to hear them more clearly. This is the only way. I pray that I do not fall asleep. When I close my eyes, I can see in another dimension. I can visualize what I hear in the spirit world, and sense the spirits in this dimension.

"They are too close to close," I mumbled. "They are on top of the roof. How did they get so close?"

I then sensed David nearby. He was worried for me, but he was not going to join the battle. Mainly because he is not a warrior and has no skills to fight them. The Demons had to be nearby, possibly before I began to pray to God. They were just too close. The enemy was not going to stop coming after me. I know they will be stopped, God's Angels will stop them.

I turned my focus on Paul, who was in the room with me. He is one of God's best Angel warriors. He is not going to let the enemy get near me, even though he wants to join the fight. He will stay by my side.

"God I need you, I need the Holy Spirit around me." Fearing it had left me, for a second.

The fighting is more intense now. More and more Demons are coming toward us. They are about a few miles away.

"Holy Spirit I need you around me about the radius around this side of town. Like the shape of a dome."

Not really sure if it was enough space. A couple of miles away, I can see the enemy is dying all around me. The enemy was getting too close to the shield. The clanging of swords all around me was very loud. They are still fighting above me.

"God, I need a five mile radius. To stop the enemy from a distance." I prayed.

The Holy Spirit is like rings around me. It seem like hours, that they have been fighting. God's Angels are fighting strongly; they are magnificent and galient. I could see them so clearly like a movie playing in my mind. This is real, and is happening in another dimension. God gave me the gift to hear what is happening in Spirit World. It all started.

#

THE YOUNG CHRISTIAN

I guess it really started in my childhood. The year was 1965. I was about eight years old at the time.

"Yola we are going to be late." My classmate shouted.

We hurried along to class, almost running to the Catholic studies building that was nearby.

It was off campus and taught by nuns during school hours.

I remember the nuns covered all in black. I always wondered why? They wore head covers and black gowns to their feet. It was a little scary to see someone wearing so much black. They taught us about baby Jesus, Mary and Joseph and some bible stories. I do not think I grasp more than that.

One time, at the age of ten years old. A group of nuns wanted to pray for me. There must have been about forty to fifty nuns or so, I do not know why they wanted to pray for me. Maybe they knew something.

I was born in Texas but raised in California. My parents were migrant workers. They came with my mother's brother to work the fields of the San Joaquin valley. My mother later got her citizenship after my father passed away. My parents took good care of us.

We never went hungry and never felt we lacked anything.

On Sundays my mother let us attend a Christian Church. I think she likes sending us off to church just to give her a break. Growing up with four sisters and two brothers you always have someone to play with and keep our mother busy.

Sunday was the day when these two sweet seventy year old ladies from church picked us up for church. Along with some of the neighborhood kids. At first, they used the church bus. But when some of the kids no longer wanted to attend. Then they used their own car.

At church, they always played the old church gospel music. How I enjoyed singing along to the old hymn book, that was the best for me. After Sunday service, the same old ladies took us to their house to have lunch with them. I remember the buttered toast bread with jelly, they served it with lunch. It tasted so delicious. My mother never made that. She always made homemade Mexican food with homemade flour tortillas.

As a teenager, I worked at a local drugstore after school in a small quiet town called San Joaquin. So I always had money for school activities. I considered myself a normal teenager, except for one day. I had started straightening out some products in the aisle when two gentlemen walked in the store and walked directly towards me.

"You young lady, we have to speak to you."

I was puzzled, I did not know them or what they wanted me for. I agreed to speak to them and walked outside with them. Nothing ever happens in this small town. It's always been quiet that I can remember and they seem harmless.

"We have traveled very far." One said. "You are with God." Said another "What."

"She is a young girl and a Mexican girl. Why her?" "You have a lot to learn." Another replied.

I did not know what to say to them and was confused by their greeting. Then they began to pray. I remember, I did not feel that it was me they were talking to, the whole time, especially when they mentioned God. It was as if they were talking to an Angel and not me.

"Where is the economy headed to?"

"Who is the richest man?" One said. They asked me a lot of questions and the only thing I do remember was a code www.

"What does that mean?" Another said.

This was the early 1970s, coming from a small town, and did not get out much. I had not heard of computers at that time. I do remember some answers coming out of my mouth. They prayed some more, outside the store. After they left, I stayed at the store a little longer. I had not completed my work hours. I was not sure I could even get back to work. But I needed the job, so I was going to try to concentrate on my work.

As I walked home that day, I started to think about the two Christians that came by and talked to me at the store. I was filled with questions. I was not sure what to make of this. I did not talk to my mother about it. I did not think she had the answers or anyone else for that matter.

In my early twenties, I got married and had two sons to a nice man who was raised as a Christian. When I met him, he was not living with his parents. It was Sunday morning, and we were all headed out to church this morning. We had been attending this christian church for some time now, but this morning it was going to be different. I was going to be baptized. I had not told my husband that I was going to be baptized. I wanted to surprise him. My husband's brother has been staying with us for a couple of weeks, since he has been in town he was going to attend church service with us.

One day, I was looking at his brother John through the screen door playing his guitar on the front porch. I wondered what he was doing here in California. He is very young, maybe sixteen years old. He still lives with his parents in Arizona. Maybe he needed to get away from the family for a while, I thought to myself. I don't think I asked my husband about it. I knew he and his brothers had a christian band back home. I have heard them play and they sound very good.

The week before the church had announced they were going to have baptism. I was looking forward to attending church for that reason. It was something I wanted to do for sometime. After accepting Jesus to be my lord and savior. I wanted to walk with God and needed to be baptized as an adult. My parents were Catholic and I was already baptized as a baby. But I wanted this as an adult. As we entered the church, the music was playing. It was old gospel hymn music. Halfway through the service the preacher makes the call.

"Does anyone want to be baptized?" He asked.

I raised my hand and walked up to the front of the church. My husband and his brother just looked at each other. I knew they were surprised. I was more a Catholic than I was a Penticostal at the time and I wanted to be in the same religion as them. This church we were attending was a Christian church and I like how they taught the word of God in the church. I wanted to attend the same church with my husband. We all got in line, then one by one as we were prayed for. When it was my turn, I looked to see if my husband was watching, as I got dunked in this tub of water. There must have been a dozen people that day that were being baptized. It was the best feeling in the world. My heart needed this, I know.

When my husband's parents came to visit us, it seems we attended more church services. A few months later, that is just what we did. My in-laws came to town from Arizona and stayed with us for a few weeks. We were all going to a small country church in one car. My husband and his parents sat in the front seat of the car, I was in the backseat with my baby. As my husband drove us there, I thought about God.

"God, I want to see you there." And that's all I said.

I didn't wait for God to answer. Because before I knew it, we were there at the Christian Church. My husband parked the car close to the church. He didn't want his parents to walk too far. As we hurried in the church, and as soon as we opened the door, almost immediately a white fog mist greeted us at the door. We stood at the entrance of the church for a few moments just enough time to look for seating. I looked around and up at the ceiling, a mist was beginning to fall on top of the people's heads. And not any lower than their heads. A beautiful cloud was hovering over the people where they were seated.

"Do you see what I see?"

My husband did not say a word. He just took my arm and walked me to the back of the church. My mother-in-law was the first to enter the church and found a seat in the front row in the middle of the aisle. The church was full of people, there was not enough seating. So we stood in the back of the church. Just then the preacher paused.

"Does anyone see what I see?" He asked in Spanish.

We raised our hands. My husband and my in-laws saw the cloud. There might have been others but I only noticed my husband and his parents raising their hands. The cloud came down over the people. This was my first witness. I do believe it was God's presence, that morning and not man made. I will always remember the day I saw God's presence there.

A couple of years later, my husband and I went through some tough times. We worked different hours and did not see each other that much. We also stopped attending church service and we argued all the time. Everything was going wrong for us. It was a very sad time in our lives. We both were not living right with God.

One late afternoon I broke down and cried. I knelt down by my bed and began to pray to the Lord. I ask God for forgiveness of all my sins. I asked Jesus to be my Lord and Savior again. I poured out my heart to the Lord.

Almost immediately, I felt a holy presence with me, it was a beautiful feeling. It was like something went through me, from the top of my head then threw my entire body. I was overcome by unimaginable love. A love for mankind that I have never felt before. The love for humanity. A love so overpowering that is hard to describe. I stayed there crying for a long time. I knew it was the presence of God I felt that day.

After that experience, I heard the spirit of the Lord so loud and clear. I did not understand the Holy Spirit and I did not know the Bible as well as I should have or what to do with the information that the Holy Spirit was given me. I went back to church to see if I could get some answers. It was not until a few months later that I found out what I was supposed to do. And that was to pray for people. Whenever the Spirit of the Lord spoke to me about people and what they were going through.

#

THE STUDIO

It was early spring, I am in my fifties now. My children are all grown up and moved away. I had just moved into an older community apartment. I like its location and the rent is priced right. I have been living alone for some time.

It was early spring and the air was cool and brisk this morning. I was looking outside the window of my small studio apartment and felt the need to pray to God. Thanking the lord for a beautiful morning he made. I was still in good health and I knew God was taking care of my children. I heard that God loves to be praised and worshiped. So I tried to please the Lord as often as I could.

My studio, besides being so small, is not as comfortable as I like it to be. But it is in a nice location of town. As I was praying, I felt I was being watched. I tried to ignore the feeling of being watched. You can always sense when someone is staring at you. There was nobody around or nearby in my studio with me. I grabbed some coffee and went back to my chair that faces the big window. I was sipping on a cup of coffee and staring out the window. There was really nothing out there to look at. Just a big tree and grass around it. As I plan my day, I continue thanking God again for all the wonderful things he has done.

"Thank you God. Thank you Jesus."

I sipped some more coffee and thought of the things I could have done differently in my life. After my divorce, I met another man that didn't work out either. I had a nice house and nice things, yet I was unhappy. When I was finally on my own, I felt happy, not bitter or mad at anyone. I forgave everyone and moved on. I had to forgive, just like

Jesus forgave. He took our sins to the cross. If I want Jesus in my life, I have to do the same.

That's why I wake up happy and wear a smile.

This morning, I thought I would head out to the gym. I found my workout clothes and got ready to go. I was going to work on my legs with weights. Going to the gym is my way of beating the disease of weak bones that my mother had. I was not given in to that disease. And I was not going to end up in a wheelchair because of Osteoporosis. I had heard it was possible for the disease to be passed on.

After the gym, I returned home to take a tub bath. My muscles were aching, I had just started weight lifting and I was out of shape. I am five feet two and about twenty pounds overweight. My leg muscles needed strength and working with weights was just the thing. My body muscles ached for months, so I was always in a bathtub. There were times, when I'd be sitting in the tub, that I get this uncomfortable feeling. I was being watched again and not just by one pair of eyes. They're watching me again. I could hear them talking to each other and they always talked to each other and never to me. At first I thought it was thin walls. After thinking about it for a while, I knew that was not the case. Almost everyone lives alone, since the complex is all studios. And the voices I hear are numerous. Of course, I even thought the office was spying on me, as strange as that sounds. But what else could it be? I was only a few months in my studio and I was already thinking of calling my friend Martha for help. I needed to know what was going on here.

I met Martha at my son's baseball practice years ago when I owned a house, out of town. Martha is in her late forties and has a nice warm face with a smile to go with it. She worries too much about everyone, especially her children. We spend time together talking about each other's family. Martha knew this town and the history of the house I was living in. Back then when I was living with the younger children's father. Martha has these unusual gifts. She can hear the Spirit of the Lord and she can see dead people. She has had these gifts for many years.

"Seeing dead people, does it not bother you?" I said. "I learned to live with it." She replied.

I cannot see dead people like Martha. I have dreams and visions of stuff that are going to happen. I guess that is the reason why I like talking to her. Weeks before a major event occured, I saw what happened, In a vision and was horrified. I prayed to God about it, that what I saw would not happen. I saw Hurricane hit an Island. And other Hurricanes doing destruction and flooding. And I was told by the Spirit of the Lord of the Earthquakes that shook the ocean floor. All these events happen either the next day or within two weeks of the visions.

Martha is the only one I can talk to about this stuff. I can talk to her about my dreams and visions. And tell her just about anything. It's not something you can talk to everybody about, because not everyone believes in the supernatural. I never spoke to my family members about the supernatural. Even though some of them are religious. I do not think they would understand. Me and Martha would sit and talk for the length of the ball game.

"I am surprised you are still there." Martha said. "People move out, as fast as they move in."

She was referring to the house I was living in. The house had strange things happening in it. It could be because it used to be a retirement home, I was told. She said people would not rent the property that long, and that she heard it had issues with spirits in the house.

I prayed for the safety of my family that God will protect us. If I forgot to say my prayers then somewhere in the middle of the night when I get up to use the restroom I'd say my prayers. I still had my faith but I was not attending church service on a regular basis at that time.

After the housing market crash we moved out of that house. It went bottom up. It was not worth half of what we bought it for and frankly, I was relieved. I wanted to get out of the relationship with the father of my younger children. We had lived there for ten years before we moved out. We found an apartment and we moved in for a short while. I wanted my son to graduate from High School, before I moved on.

The day finally came, my son went to live in the Dorms of the college he was going to attend. Years earlier, I had made up my mind, I was going to leave my children's father after they all grew up. I was not going to spend the rest of my life unhappy with someone who I did not love anymore. Plus he was a difficult man to live with.

I called my friend Martha and told her I was going to pick her up for lunch. Martha's family has only one car and the family needs it. After lunch, I invited her to my studio. I wanted her to see them, if she could. I told Martha of the feeling I was getting, of being watched and hearing voices.

"Do you think someone is spying on me? Their voices sound like young men." I said. "They are not spies but Spirits." she said.

I never heard Spirits voices before. Not even when I was living in that house, where Mary saw dead Spirits. The only voice I ever heard years ago was the Spirit of the Lord and that was different. Mary could tell me what they looked like and where in the house they were, sometimes that creeped me out, but I was never afraid.

"I have been praying a lot, seeking God. I have been reading the Bible and attending church service on a regular basis" I said.

"What church?"

"It is nearby here, a Christian Church. It just seems strange that I can hear people talking." I said.

"How do you do that Martha?" "Not talk to them." "I just ignore them."

For Martha, this has been going on since she was a child. She was always praying and asking God for help at a young age. She had questions that she needed help with. And ever since then, she has been able to see dead people and Angels at certain times in her life. I took Martha back home after her short visit. While driving Martha back home I began to pray to God.

"God help me with the things I cannot see, especially these voices that sound so clear and the things I can."

After talking to Martha, I had a better understanding of what was going on in my place. I decided I was going to ignore them.

#

One evening, I wanted to go out but not alone. I called my sister Rachel to accompany me.

I was spending too much time at home. She agreed and came over the next evening. Rachel is a hard worker and no longer married. She said she would call me when she was nearby. I hurried to meet her outside while she was parking her car. It was late in the evening when she arrived. We decided to take my car and drive to the restaurant.

The restaurant bar attracts the older couples, who are in their forties and older. Sometimes when my brother and sisters come into town, they like to go out to the club to catch up with the family. And this is one of their favorite places to go. My sister and I had fun. Of course we danced alone without a partner, but then, everyone there seemed to be dancing without partners.

The next morning, I felt terrible. I woke up sick, my stomach hurt and I could not get out of bed. It must have been the fish I ate that night before, and not the one drink of wine I had. That one drink could not have gotten me sick, it had to be the fish. I had left it in the car for a couple of hours, before I remembered that I left groceries in the back seat. I was nauseous, I had not felt this sick in a long time. I could not even get out of bed, my stomach hurt so much. Just then, my phone started ringing and buzzing. It was about eight in the morning. The guy I gave my phone number to, was texting me. He wanted to go out for lunch. I was not going anywhere.

"No, I texted back. "I am too sick, sorry.

He texted me some more and I texted the same thing back.

"Some other time I texted back." He was persistent, that's for sure.

I could hear the young spirits so clearly, talking to each other about me. "She looks sick." One said.

"She has botulism." Another said.

They sounded almost concerned. It was late in the evening when I threw up the fish. I felt I was going to die from food poison. The next morning, I felt a little better, yet still weak. I later called my sister. I wanted to tell her what happened to me. And that the guy I gave the number to, was texting me all morning long.

"I probably would have gone out with him, had I not gotten sick." I said.

"That is why, I never give out my number. There are guys that just do not stop calling." She said,

I did not tell her of the voices in my studio. My sister would not understand nor believe me. The last thing I needed was for her to tell my other sisters and brothers. Oh yeah, I could hear it now.

"Yola has lost it." They would have said.

I hung up the phone and sat outside the patio. I did not feel like doing much that evening. I guess I was still recovering.

#

One night about eleven p.m. I could not go to sleep so I set up my easel. I thought I would start with clouds. Painting clouds always took too much time, figuring them out and capturing the depth in them. They seem mysterious at times. I finally got the shapes of the clouds, when I heard a voice In my ear.

"Fire." The voice said. "Fire." I heard the voice in my ear again.

I have never thought of painting fire in my clouds, I thought. At that moment the phone rang.

"Mr. Jones' house is on fire." The caller said.

It was a friend of mine who called. I put my brushes down and rushed over to the house. I could not get close enough. When I arrived there, the street was blocked. The fire was up ahead. There was already a fire truck, and an officer not letting anyone get near the house. I parked a little ways off and walked the rest of the way. A Lady there was talking about what had happened, she heard an explosion and rushed outside with Mr.

Jones. I was glad Mr. Jones got out safely. The next morning, I began to think about God and how he spoke to me in my ear. Wow, how awesome was that. It made me happy that the Spirit of the Lord was speaking to me again. God was telling me to pray for someone. It caught me by surprise. It has been a while since I heard God's voice. I guess I should have prayed.

When I hear the Spirit of the Lord. I was supposed to act upon it and pray immediately. About two weeks later, I heard what happened to Mr. Jones' house. Apparently, the fire was due to electrical wiring in one of the rooms and the explosion was from the liquor bottles getting hot.

I have been living alone now for about four years. I was happy and enjoyed my time reading, and doing my favorite things such as painting, taking drives to the coast.

I enjoyed going to church and listening to the word of God.

At my studio, the young Spirits were still talking to one another and never spoke to me. I'd be watching TV and still hear them talking to each other. They comment on what I was watching on the set. And sometimes, they change the channel on me. That always frustrated me. I still could not see them, just hear them. One day, I just got mad.

"This is my studio! I pay rent here! Stop changing the channels!" I shouted.

They did not listen, so I went outside to take a walk. When I was back inside my apartment, I could hear them greet each other. A young Spirit named David is the one I heard the most. They all greeted him when he entered the studio. They were harmless and annoying spirits. The only strange thing is that they were dead and I could hear them. I was never scared of them, at any time. Maybe because I felt I could always call on the Lord. I remember reading in the Bible "whom shall I fear," that was enough for me not to be afraid. And because I haved lived in a haunted house for more than ten years. Through the years, I relied on my faith that Jesus would take care of everything. I only feared the lord.

2 Timothy 1;7/ Luke 1;50

I woke up this morning planning to visit my friend Martha. Driving to her house I began to praise and worship God. It was always the best time to talk to the lord.

"God you shine. You made a beautiful morning. Look at it. It's just so beautiful."

Usually after it rains the clouds are beautiful to look at. I parked the car and stared at the clouds. Anywhere I had to be, I could wait. I thought to myself. I wonder how the Lord made the Earth. God did beautiful work. I was just awed about it. God never really answered me that day. But I always spoke to the Lord.

As I was driving I remembered that on the weekends, when my daughter was still living with me, we always took drives into town.

"You pray too much. Are your eyes closed mama?" My daughter said,

"No, I don't close my eyes when I drive. I may be praying, but with my eyes open." I said.

I have never talked to my daughter or sons of what God lets me hear in the spirit world. They knew I was a Christian but that is all they knew. As I was driving to Martha's house. I was thinking of the young Spirits there, they are not so bad. Trying to find the good in a bad situation. I greeted Martha from the street. She came outside to open the gate as her dogs were barking up a storm.

"Hey Bud, How are you? I said.

"It's good to see you. Come in. What's going on with you?" Martha said. "Will you know, dead spirits? The usual."

Martha has a nice house with Angels figures everywhere . Her house is small but cozy. I was glad she was alone. Sometimes her family is home, but they never seem to mind that me and Martha talk about supernatural things.

We talk about the Bible and our faith too. Then she offered her great breakfast of beans, country potatoes and eggs. I always loved Martha's beans.

"Martha, I can not get used to living with Spirits. Do you know, they are holding my T.V. hostage. They just change the channels on me, and they talk all night long. I am trying to deal with this bad situation. They're terrible. Sometimes, I have to go outside, to get away from them. But that does not help, because more spirits come. At least, I can not see them. I think everything would have been fine, had I not yelled at them to leave me alone." I said.

"Stop talking to them." She said,

We talked a little more about our lives and the children. It was getting late in the day. I told Martha I needed to get home. I thanked her. Talking to Martha always seems to help. As I was driving home,

I thought about the one bedroom apartment across the street that was for rent. It's a bigger place for my paintings. The next day, I went to see the lady at the rental office.

"You can rent it for just a little more than what you're paying for the studio. " The lady said.

"Okay, I'll take it."

I never went to see the inside of the apartment. It was blocked off that day. They must have been painting it. I looked at it from the outside and it looked fine. Before I knew it, I was moving in. I just needed to clean the studio that I was leaving. After I moved all my things into my new one bedroom apartment I went back to clean the studio. I left the door open while I was cleaning. I did not know how the spirits would take it, me moving out. I cleaned the place for hours. And did not want the office to charge me more money. Even though the spirits were harmless, I needed to be alone. I had hoped that would be the last time I heard them. I gave it one last look at the place and left.

The one bedroom apartment felt cold and unsettling, not right. It didn't feel right. Almost immediately, I heard them there too. But these were different, they were more like rebellious rebel types and more aggressive. They never scared me. It had to be my faith. The other place they did not scare me either, they just annoyed me. These were not just annoying but wicked and evil by the sound of their voices. Their voices sounded of young and old people. I tried to get on with my life and daily routine. It was not easy, this place had a problem too. I know, I should have walked in the apartment and checked things out before moving in..

After a couple of weeks, I did not want to be at home. I'd go to the gym, the mall, the recreation room anywhere and stay longer than I have to. I found things to do all day. Just so that I did not have to be home. I tried to ignore them, it's just that they are so loud and clear and there are so many of them. It was like a bunch of uninvited people living with me and they seem to want to harm me. Just by their voices thou never talked to me just to each other.

One evening out of boredom I decided to go to the casino. I did not want to stay at my apartment any longer of course. As I was getting dressed, I thought of the harmless Spirits at the other studio. Maybe, I should have not been thinking of the kids from the other Studio, but I couldn't help but wonder how they died. They just did not know they were dead. Maybe I should learn more about this. And why, they were not in Heaven and hanging around on Earth. What happened to them?

"Kid"

"David, I am going to the casino." First I said it out loud then I thought.

That was weird, why the kid? To tell you the truth, I did not feel right, asking or even thinking about the young spirit. Was it because, when I was ill in bed, his voice is who I heard the most. Like concern or something? I want to say again. I did not feel right in my heart, asking spirit David to go to the casino. Spirit David's voice sounded like he was in his early twenties.

"What?" he shouted in a loud voice. I heard his feet pound the floor when he came to the living room of my apartment. He had heard me. Again, I did not feel right in my heart like a tugging of sort.

I did not fear David or anyone in the apartment. I had to know more of this supernatural world they were living in. I finished doing my make-up and brushed my hair. It was quiet in my car, as I drove to the casino. I did not put any music on. I guess I wanted to hear David. He did not say a word. I knew he was with me. The casino was busy as usual, I found a penny machine, and played it all night long. Until I lost sixty dollars, it was time to go. The drive home was no different than the drive up.

The next day, I drove to check on a friend to see how he was doing. He was an elderly gentleman who looked like he could not take care of himself.

As I was driving over to visit. I heard David with another spirit in my car, they had followed me, it's not hard for dead spirits to follow anybody anywhere. After making sure the elderly gentleman ate something. I went to the living room to read my Holy Bible. As I was reading the scriptures, I sensed that David came around and got close to me. I was not sure why he got close to me and made me uncomfortable. I think he wants to hear me read. So I read long enough and loud enough so he could hear the word of God. I have noticed that Spirits like hanging around restrooms.

The dead like to look at people using the toilet and taking showers. And that is just what they did, anywhere I went, any establishment, there were Spirits, especially in restrooms. And of course, David was there too.

Spirits have no regard for who you are. Spirits do gross things to people in the toilets after they use them and because they are Spirits, people never feel anything. All this is going on in another dimension called the spirit world. No, I did not have to tell you this. But I thought you should know this too.

All this I heard in the Supernatural world. I hear and see in my vision. In just weeks, I've come to realize that the dead spirits walk around in our world, in another dimension. It is very strange for me. And wondered why God lets me hear the Spirit World? One evening, sitting on the edge of my bed, I asked David about his past life.

"How did you die?"

"I do not know." He replied. I think I caught him off guard. Because he left. You see people did not talk to the dead probably because they do not hear them. When he returned, he told me how he died.

"Me and my brothers were out hunting and one of them accidentally shot me. I remember my mother crying a lot for me." He said.

David died around the year 1854 and did not remember much after that. David was in his early twenties when he died. He has been in the studio that I left, ever since.

"I was afraid to leave the studio." David said.

I could not help but feel sorry for the kid. After our talk, I carried on with my daily activities.

I was beginning to understand why God did not want me to talk to spirits. Spirits like to stick around you like glue. David was doing just that. I ask God for forgiveness, for talking to Spirit David. He'd follow me around everywhere I went. I did not like that. I went to see a friend one day. The kid followed me there too. Everywhere, he followed me to the gym, to the coffee shop, everywhere. Boy! Did I open a can of worms? So to speak. It was my fault for talking to David. Had I listened to Martha, I would not be in this mess that I was in.

"Don't talk to spirits." Martha said.

There was not a day that went by, that I did not ask God for forgiveness, for talking to David. At the time, I felt so guilty I did not realize that God had already forgiven me,the first time I asked. In Jesus name.

Before I entered a room or a house I always said a prayer. For God to protect me and watch over me, while I was in their home. I had to pray, I was able to hear Spirits, everywhere I went. They were not the same ones either. Spirits were everywhere. Soon as I open the door, here comes David and his mother figure. She was not his real mother.

But I will call her his mother figure. Only because she was always consulting him.

Thinking back now, she may have been a witch. But I did not know that at the time. It was very annoying, David following me around. I shouted at the Spirit to stop following me around, but it fell on deaf ears. If I went to the toilet, to the car, to the gym. He'd followed me.

I kept praying to God that David would stop following me around. I needed to figure this out. What was I saying wrong? That my prayers were not being answered. When I went to visit people. There he was, in the kitchen at my friend's house. Talking with his mother figure in the kitchen.

My prayers must have been blocked by him, it had to be. Other prayers God answered. But when it came to David, it seems they were blocked. I believe that if you ask God for anything, he will answer your prayers. I was getting desperate, I was going to have David tide and bind. I asked God to tie and bind David. The Lord heard my prayers.

"God tied and bound David with ropes." In Jesus name. I asked. He was tied and bound. I could hear him shouting.

"Let me go, let me go!" He shouted.

Good, I thought. He was not going to follow me anymore. But what was I going to do with him? I can not just leave him in the kitchen. Before I knew it, his mother figure walks up to him and releases the ropes. Ropes might not have been a good idea. I was going to have to give it more thought. I finished cleaning the house. And of course, spirit David followed me back to my apartment. He found a way to get in my car.

Reading my Bible is peaceful. I needed the word of God and I wanted to learn how to battle evil, if I needed to. It was getting bad in my apartment and I knew eventually, I'd need to call on God to cast out spirits and evil spirits. I read the scripture Luke 10:19. Then I ask God to cast out all spirits out of my Apartment in Jesus name. As I tapped my bible two times. Spirits you are rebuked cast out of this apartment in Jesus name.

"Get out, you are cast out."

The spirits left after they were rebuked in the name of Jesus. The more I read the Bible and listen to the word of God the more my faith was growing. I was exercising my faith. The dead were everywhere. I could see it in my mind and visions of the dead walking the earth. I could hear them nearby, anywhere I went. There they were, the dead walking the Earth without a skeleton, only their spirit. Just like the living carrying on, so do the dead.

Except it is more wicked and weird to say the least. But they were dead and did not realize who they were or what they were. If you can imagine a horror movie. That's how it is. There are evil spirits in the corner streets making spirits do whatever they want them to do.

I had walked into another dimension. I was still living but could hear the dead spirits everywhere I went. The worst is that evil ran rapidly in this Dimension. There was a lot of prostitution in spirit world. They raped the living, because the living can't feel that they are doing that. And they did a lot worse things to the living. The spirits get into your thoughts and use your fears. It is very bad here in the spirit world. The spirits use freeways, just like us. They use spirit vehicles in their dimension. Or they jump from vehicle to vehicle while in motion in the living world. We share the same planet with the spirits.

Occasionally I pray to God to get me out of the spirit world. I see and hear too much, when I close my eyes. I do not like the spirit world. My faith keeps me alive in this world. They will grow on your fears if you let them. I never was afraid of them. I am not sure why. I had my faith in God and his son Jesus. That's how I stayed alive. If evil spirits get too close. I asked God to protect me, in Jesus name. I believe that God protects me.

I am not afraid of them. It was just dealing with them on a daily basis. Living in two worlds is not easy.

This morning, I was going to check up on a friend who needed help with cooking and cleaning. He could not cook for himself or much of anything else. While dinner was cooking slowly, I went to the living room and opened my Holy Bible to read the scriptures. I am still determined to read more chapters. Of course David was nearby, he liked to hear me read the word. And I did find it odd that he liked to hear me read.

After dinner and making sure my friend ate his meal. I cleaned up the house for him. I still had laundry to do. After putting a load of laundry in the washing machine. I went to another room to relax. I got a little sleepy after reading my bible, I had not planned to fall asleep as I laid on the floor. The room was empty and it had no furniture. I was awakened by a sharp pain on my back. Jane the spirit had stabbed me on my back. David was nearby and saw what happened.

"Why did you do that?" He said, to the female spirit.

The female spirit did not have an answer. But listening to Jane talk in the past, I knew she was crazy and not in her right mind. Just then God put a thought in my head. To tap my back three times to the floor. I did just that. I did not know why or what it was for, at the time. The next morning, I felt something weird on my back. It felt like it was not of this world, but evil. I ask God to take it out. I did not know how to deal with this. My back needed a special prayer and faith to cast out spirits of this kind. So this weird feeling went on for months.

I wanted to ask the church for prayer. But I needed to find the right church that knew how to cast out spirits. I was still learning the word of God, and I did not feel qualified to cast out spirits from myself.

One evening I drove to the coffee shop, I really wanted to use the internet there. As I was driving to my destination, I heard them talking, David and Jane the spirits. David is in his twenties and Jane in her teens.

I did not invite them to come along. I must have had a bad morning when I yelled at them.

"Get out of my car." I shouted.

I think I even cursed at them. They were crying when I stopped yelling at them. "God forgive me for that." praying to the Lord.

But not to be left alone, for not even a second of my life. Spirits are always around me. It's just a little too much. Everywhere I went, David followed me. I was very upset with them, that I had to yell at them. As I walked back to my apartment. I heard a loud howl coming from David, his feelings were hurt. He sounded sort of like a wounded animal. But it was more like a wicked eerie howl. I had to apologize to the spirit kids. I did later that evening.

A couple of days later, I met up with a Church friend. I did not tell her about my back problem. I did not think she would be able to help me anyway. She had a message for me, from God.

"What is it?" I said.

"God told me, to tell you, not to yell at the kids" She said.

"What kids?" Then it dawned on me. "Oh my." I said. The only kids I yelled at were the spirit kids that were in my car.

The next day, my guy friend called and texted me that he was coming over that day. The message was two days old. It was a voice message. My cell phone was jacked, held hostage by David. I see I have a bigger problem. Why would he mess with my phone unless he was jealous of my friend. I was furious.

"Leave me alone. Go away." I shouted.

He is a very stubborn spirit. I still need to learn a lot more on how to deal with annoying spirits.

There is a fight going on between good and evil. The more I knew God's word the better I was in dealing with situations of the supernatural. I drove to visit a friend, to clean his house. And of course, David followed me there and some Spirits from my apartment.

Most of the time, there were spirits in the house already. So I pray before I enter any house.

These Spirits in my one-bedroom apartment were into white slavery. The spirits are not just spirits but evil spirits. The spirits were running an evil business there. They were trying to take the souls of young people. From what I could hear they appear at people's home and take their souls from young men women and children and sell them for prostitution.

They run a sex trafficking business at one of the bedroom apartment. All this is going on in the spirit world. The evil spirits enter into people's homes and hide in couches, seats, bags just about anything. These are some ways they enter people's lives.

The sex traffickers will try to sell their souls to buyers around the world. Again, all this is happening in the supernatural world. They had even tried to sell me. I spend a lot of time fighting them with prayers, God scriptures and faith. I ask God to tie and bind the spirits with ties and binds from Heaven. That no Spirit can release the ties and binds put on from Heaven. This went on for a couple of weeks. I had lost a lot of sleep. At night, I relied on faith that God will protect me from these evil buyers. There were times, I asked God to make me invisible to Spirits so that I did not have to deal with evil spirits around me. I believed I was invisible to spirits. I realize this is now a third dimension in the spirit world. Where they can not see you.

After weeks of no sleep, I had enough. I was going to exercise my faith. I asked God to destroy the organization of sex trafficking and release the young people from the buyers, that were being held against their will.

Once their souls were released, I asked God to send his Angels to guide them back to their homes. I also asked God to erase the evil spirits' memories of me and everything they knew about me. All the people they had taken captive, we're now set free. All this I heard in the supernatural world. Praise the Lord thank you Jesus.

One day, I was driving to the store to get some groceries and felt smothered by David. It has been about a couple of months now that I have been annoyed by the spirit David. I was not feeling good about the situation I got myself in. David felt like something you cannot shake off, like a bad stain on your clothing. No, this was far worse. David and another Spirit were in my car. I was not having a good day.

"Stop following me!" I shouted.

I carried a Spirit cloth in my car. That I got through prayer. Which is really the Holy Spirit. I got so mad that I started waving it around in the car. I must have cut him up with the prayer cloth. Because I could hear some moaning.

"David is hurt." A spirit said. The moaning came from the floor of the car. "Stay there and do not move." I said.

I did not see the spirit. But I knew in my mind that he was in bad shape. I ran inside to my apartment and picked up my Bible and read a few scriptures. I asked God, if it be your will, to make David whole again. In Jesus name. God answered my prayer, he made David whole again. I had never prayed for a spirit before. After that, David went inside the apartment. I could hear him, he was talking to his friends. I never used the spirit cloth again. I thank God and Jesus for making things possible.

One evening, I was sitting on the bench outside my apartment. when a friend of mine stops by, to talk to me. It was my friends that lived in the complex.

"I'm attending a Revival and would like for you to attend." She said, "Oh I love to go."

She gave me the time and place to attend. I have been wanting to attend a Revival for so long. I could not wait to go. I wanted to be with fellow Jesus believers like myself. I was so happy to be at the Revival. We worship for at least an hour. Then he began preaching. The Evangelist prayed for me and others, toward the end of the service. The service at times smelled of a forest after a rain shower. It was a beautiful smell of morning dew. It was God's presence.

After attending service three weeks straight, I was heavily anointed. It's like being drunk, but in the spirit. The lady who asked me to attend the Revival is the same lady I asked to come by my apartment. She came by the same day I asked her to come over. I wanted her to see if she had an idea what was going on at my place. The lady came by the house that afternoon. After walking very quietly inside the house.

"I need to pray for your home, there is a big hole in this wall" Pointing to a wall that my couch was leaning on. The size of the hole was six by eight feet wide. I was very creeped out about this.

"Evil is around this wall." She said,

It was not a hole that I could literally see. But as a Christian I could understand that it was Supernatural. Now I understand why this place felt wicked. I did not fear them, but felt disturbed by the fact they were in my apartment. We talked a little about ourselves. And before she left, we prayed for my apartment. I thank her for coming.

At night, I could hear the spirits talking to each other. I prayed to the Lord, to shield me from all evil. In my spirit, the Lord told me to move out. I realize I moved in quickly without consulting God. I should have consulted the Lord in the first place. I gave the rental office my thirty-day notice that I was moving out.

The rental office was surprised that I was moving out so quickly since I only lived there two months. The next two weeks, I went to stay at my sister and then my best friend's home. I did not want to sleep in my place anymore. When it was a moving day, I could not get my stuff out fast enough. I felt the Lord tell me to get out as quickly as possible. As I was moving boxes to the rental truck. All of a sudden, I felt dizzy. I got hit on the head by a spirit. I asked for healing from God. And to tie and bind the spirit who hurt me. They were going to be tied up until I could get all my stuff out.

I cleaned out the refrigerator, and donated the canned goods to the community center. I moved my stuff to the storage unit. I had not found a place to stay. I just wanted to move out as soon as possible. I went back to my friend Martha and stayed at her place for a couple of nights. I told her of the weird stuff going on in my apartment. But not of the sex traffickers in the spirit world and the loud growl I heard one night. I just did not want to spend another night there. I want to say that I was not scared but more uneasy about my living situation. Spirits are one thing, but evil spirits are another. And I was not ready for a battle I was not prepared for at that time.

"Martha, I hope it's okay with you and your husband. He's not going to mind? Is Juan okay about it? I said.

"Don't worry about it." She said,

I was happy to stay with them for a couple of nights. It was getting to be too much for me. Her couch was going to be just fine. In just four days, I found a place to stay. I answered an ad for a roommate. I did not have money for an apartment just for myself. I made the call. And a young man answered.

"Are you the one renting a room? "Yes," He replied.

"When can I see it?" "Tomorrow is fine."

He sounded very young. After briefly talking to him we agreed to meet at a diner. That day I drove up early to meet him. He looked very handsome driving up in his car.

"Are you the lady looking for a room? "Yes, that's me." I said.

"Are you Jose?" "Yes, follow me."

I followed him in my car. The apartment was nice. There was a picture of the Virgin Mary on the wall. And he seems to be a very nice young man with good moral values. The fact he was still attending college, that told me he needed to rent the room fast.

"The last person I rented the room to, did not work out. The noise of the train going by at night bothered him"

The train was not going to be a problem for me. I was just glad the age difference did not bother him. I also did not tell him I was employed. I rented the room and moved in right away. Within two weeks, I got a job with a company down the street. I just needed to work. When you share an apartment, money seems to go further.

THE GATHERING

It was late November, my family usually gets together for the holidays. This was no exception. They arrived early into town and wanted to catch up with everyone. They were going to meet at a restaurant. For me to go out and meet them there, it's going to be a little bit of a challenge. I asked God that I wanted to meet up with my brothers and sisters. And that I needed spirits cast out from the area. I prayed, before I headed out there to meet with them. I asked God to keep all Spirits away from the restaurant by placing the Holy spirit shield around the restaurant about five hundred feet away for the duration I was there. In Jesus name. I did not want to battle unless I had to. I was not sure I could ask God for his shield around the place.

To battle for me, was to be ready if I was under attack. God sends Angels to fight my battle. The thing is, I wanted to enjoy the evening. And not be on guard. God answered my prayers, everything went fine. I arrived at about nine p.m. We all sat outside by the fireplace. It was keeping us warm out there. The event was fun and was nice knowing that the spirits were not going to be in the restaurant.

Spirits are not my biggest problem, but the evil ones. I had to be on guard at all times and be ready for anything. I did not want to be slain in the spirit. And too many Spirits attract evil spirits. I wanted to enjoy my time with my family. And not have to listen to what was around me. Spirits only bothered me, but I was not sure if they were going to bother my brothers or sisters.

They are very social people, they like to dance and have fun. Though they are in their fifties they do look like they could pass for their forties.

They take good care of themselves. We enjoyed each other's company and danced to old sixties and seventies music known as old school. I left at about eleven p.m. It was a cool night out. The valley never gets that cold. I went home and thanked God for a good evening with my family.

I woke up feeling good about everything. After praising God for good morning, I made my way to the toilet and dealt with Spirits there. As I mentioned before, Spirits like hanging around in restrooms. My thoughts were on Thanksgiving dinner. I needed to prepare something for tonight. I just hope it was going to be as nice as the pre-celebration at the restaurant. There was still the problem with David the spirit, he was going to follow me there.

David moved into my apartment. He was infatuated with me, I did not see the young man that way. I told him that. It's as though he did not care what I said or what I thought of him. When I went to bed he was there, when I woke up, he was there. He would not leave me alone. His friends were now dropped by, like if it was David's place and they were there visiting him.

Even though I would cast out dead spirits out of my house day and night, more would return. It was bad at night, it was hard getting any sleep. I lay in bed for hours. But I could hear them talking all night long. It was like having an uninvited guest in your home not wanting to leave. Sometimes when I would get up in the middle of the night I 'd cast out spirits. I read the scripture from the Bible Luke 10:19 kjv, behold I give you the authority to tread on serpents and scorpions, and over all the power of the enemy: and nothing shall by any means hurt you.

"I demand you spirits in the name of Jesus to get out of my home. You Spirits are rebuked."

And then I tap my Bible twice to cast out spirits in the name of Jesus. If they were in the house. the spirits have to obey in Jesus' name. I did not like spirits talking all night long.

Whenever I use the toilet. David disrespected me. I was tired of David disrespecting me. That's when I asked God to make David stop. David was told by the Spirit of the Lord to stop, but in less than a day he was at it again. He would not listen. I asked God again, that David was still doing what he was not supposed to do.

Well before I knew it, in a split of a second God's Angels were here in my room. They grabbed a hold of David, and cut off his penis. I could hear David yell in pain. David was mad at me. If David cried, I could not hear him. David got very angry with me.

"You are going to pay for this." He said.

I knew he was going after my family for revenge. I told God of David's threat and for God to place angels and warriors to protect my family. God's angels were always steps ahead of evil doers like David. God protected my family and always after that. Jesus is protecting them. That is what I believe. In the supernatural world and the natural world. David was still in my home, he was not going to leave. David was turning evil, and he was dark. Right about this time, I sensed his mother figure in the room. She, too, did not want to spend the entire day with David. This evil spirit David followed me around for two days. I did not want to speak to him, in this form he was in. David was evil, as darkness was. One night, I just had to say something.

"You know you're going to the Lake of Fire where you will be tormented day and night." I said. David was a Demon. He only had evil thoughts of hurting someone.

"You will get no rest day or night." I said.

Just then, he began to cry. "I do not want to go to the Lake of Fire. " He said.

All those times I was reading the Bible out loud, David was listening. He learned something from listening to me read. I felt sorry for David, he was a spirit at one time. His only crime at the time was that he was infatuated with me.

"Pray to God for forgiveness and in Jesus name" I said.

I heard David pray out loud to God, Just then, a beautiful thing happened. God turned David back to a spirit. He was no longer a Demon. David did not ask for his penis. But God gave him that back too. He also had no lust for me anymore. All this I saw in the supernatural world. Glory to God. Hallelujah

For the next couple of weeks it was not so bad with David's presence in my apartment, he did not bother me anymore. There were still spirits in my apartment day and night. Some dropped by to visit David and talk all night long with them. There are spirits everywhere I go. Not that they followed me, they are just there on earth.

Not to mention all the females, these guys brought with them. The female Spirits like David a lot. They were always looking for him. The spirits like watching me do anything. Sometimes David went out with a female Spirit, he did not stay away long. The only good thing was, David did not have any desire for me. I still feel him staring at me at night, while I am trying to get some sleep.

In the middle of the night when I use the restroom, or even when I am sitting in the toilet, I ask God to cast out Spirits, in Jesus name. I do not trust them, and do not want them around.

I drive daily to my job nearby. Dead spirits are everywhere, and this job site was no exception. I was working at the office, when I was attacked by an evil spirit. It came from the second floor. I was cut on my face. Just then the spirit of the Lord spoke to me.

"Pray, you have internal bleeding" The Spirit of the Lord said. I ran to the bathroom to pray. I began to pray there, while waiting in line. The restroom stalls were full.

"Are you alright?" The girl asked. That was standing near me. "Yes, I'm praying"

I prayed for healing. I did not care who saw me praying. I just did not want to be disturbed. I did not care if I got fired from this job. This was my life. As I prayed, I wanted to remember all those times God healed me. I was not bleeding inside anymore. Thank-you Jesus.

Just then David shows up in my bathroom stall. I did not want to be bothered by him. I prayed for David to leave. He did not leave, not even after my prayers for him to leave. Just then a God's warrior shows up and puts a sword at David.

"Did you pray against the ladies' prayers?" The warrior Angel asked.

I prayed fast, for David not to get hurt. David was inches away from dying from the sword of the warrior.

"Do not pray against the ladies' prayers." The warrior said. "That is meant for God."

I did not want him to die just because he did not know. I prayed for David so that he would not die. To die again in the spirit world and is evil, is to be sent to Sheol. I walk back to my desk. I knew I was going to be alright. As for David, he learned a valuable lesson. I realize now, why God never answered my prayers. David intercepted my prayers to God.

David almost died in the spirit world by God's warrior. So that is why, I could never get David to stop following me around. My prayers were intercepted. God's warriors will kill the spirits that Intercept the prayers that are meant for God. Now I know. I am not saying, this is the same for everyone. This is what I heard, in the spirit world.

There were nights I was attacked in my sleep. If I forgot to pray before I fell asleep. I was either stabbed or cut in some part of my body. Sometimes the female Spirits cut my buttocks. I do not know why they did this. Other than that, I heard them say that they like them. One evening, I heard something wrestling outside. There was someone outside or something. I felt I was in danger, my heart started racing. The enemy was close by. David and some of the spirits were in my room.

"David." I said. "I hear something outside."

In my vision, I could see someone or something. It was getting closer and closer to my room. I sensed it was evil. David went outside to see if he could stop what was coming. I could hear and see it in my mind. I closed my eyes to get a better picture of it. It was dark all around. Then I saw David. David was fighting the enemy, hand-to-hand combat.

David has no experience in fighting. David is fighting a Demon outside my apartment. I prayed to God for a warrior. I heard when the warrior arrived.

"David, move out of the way, I got this." The warrior Angel said.

It was a trained Assassin Demon. The Assassin was after me. The Angel warrior thrust his sword at the assassin and killed him. And drag the spirit to Sheol. David was no match for the Assassin. I had not realized how much David cared. I was thankful he fought for me. David was very brave that night. I did not know, I was in so much danger. I should have started praying sooner. I thank David for fighting my battle. It did not change anything between us. When it was time to go to bed, I felt okay about sleeping. I said my prayers and fell asleep.

One day I was moving my stuff out of my son's car to my home. I had left my car at his place, so that I could move some of my stuff from his garage. His car could hold more stuff than my two seater car. I was walking up to the door of my apartment when all of a sudden, I got hit hard on my chest. It felt sharp as if I were stabbed. I sat down for a moment on the couch. I told my son I was not going back to get my car.

"I will call you tomorrow." I said. "What's wrong mama? Jacob said.

I did not tell my son about the pain I was feeling. How can I tell my son of the pain I was feeling in my spirit.

"I guess I'm tired, I need prayer." I said. "I'll be fine." When my son left, I went to my room to lay down on my bed and tried to pray.

I got my laptop and placed it on my bed and played Christian music. I needed to hear my special song playing, while I worship God. I could not raise my hands to worship, for the pain in my heart was strong. As I laid on the bed and thought of my children. What could I say to them? It's something they could not understand. This is happening in Supernatural and it was happening to me.

As I was praying, I was getting very sleepy. I do not think I'm going to be able to stay awake. I need to stay awake. must pray to God. I was alone, with no one to pray for me. I was fighting to stay awake. I knew my prayers were being answered but I was just too sleepy to stay awake and pray for myself for healing.

David was by my side, he knew it was bad. I was stabbed in my heart. I tried to pray for myself. But I was just too drowsy. I did pray a little here and there. That God will heal my heart. Just then, I noticed his mother figure's presence in the room.

"She's dying David." She said,

David howld, like something wounded, out of sorrow. I could hear spirits talking all around my room. I continued to pray. I was so tired, it was getting harder to stay awake.

"I brought a doctor." A spirit said.

Oh my. I thought. They're not going to do what I think they're going to do? At that moment, I began to pray. This time I knew what I needed.

"God of Abraham, Isaac and Jacob, God of Moses, you are the All Mighty God. You are the creator of Heaven and Earth. I need your help in Jesus' name." I said.

"God, I need a surgeon from Heaven. In Jesus name." I asked. One came down instantly, I could hear him. It was one of God's beautiful Angels.

"It looks like healing has already commenced, but it needs a little more work,"The Angel Surgeon said.

The Angel Surgeon got David to help with the surgery. I could not stay awake. At one point, I fell asleep and began to dream. In my dream I was opening a gate and it was beautiful. I was sooo.... close to opening the gate. I was just inches away. Just then, I opened my eyes. The surgeon was still working on my heart. I closed my eyes again to see what was going on. By closing my eyes I can hear and see better in the spirit world. David had my heart in his hands. He was helping the surgeon that came from Heaven.

"God send me another surgeon and Assistant." I asked. In Jesus name.

I knew David cared, But for these things, a surgeon is better. David did not have to help anymore. There were two Angels from Heaven working on my heart.

"I had her heart in my hands." David said.

I then dozed off again. It seemed like seconds. The surgery was over. There were a lot of spirits that evening. I could hear David telling them to get back. The spirits that were there that evening witnessed theAngels come down from heaven to perform surgery on me. They were not going to be the same again. And neither was I.

The spirits ask David how they can be saved. David helped the spirits with that. He showed them how to pray and ask for forgiveness. David was praying for the spirits to be saved. I do not know more than what I heard. That same night, God did something beautiful that I will never forget. God gave David wings.   That was a surprise for me. I was happy for David. He was now one of God's Angels. I know Angels are made not born. But God can do anything, and David got wings. I thanked God for healing me by sending his Angels down from Heaven. I went to sleep.

The next morning, I was feeling very good about things. Just the fact the Lord's Angels came down to perform surgery to my heart, and everything about last night was just glorious.

"Glory to God in the highest hallelujah hallelujah. Praise the Lord. Thank you Jesus." I shouted. "It is a glorious morning, God you Shine."

I was so happy about things. I felt blessed. Later on in the day, I thought of looking for a job. I opened my laptop, to see where I was going to apply for work. I wanted to work in another town. Maybe as an esthetician. There were still spirits in the house, and it seemed like more of them. Since I did not like spirits in the house and they attract evil spirits. It was time to cast out spirits as soon as possible. Dealing with David was enough, I do not fear spirits or evil spirits. I have God and his Son Jesus. Praise the Lord.

I thought about the surgery again, and David becoming an Angel. How awesome was that. He has girlfriends spirits that look for him on a daily basis. They are going to be in for a big surprise. David must have been very good looking because the female Spirits were always coming by looking for him. They always ask the spirits where he is at.

David still comes around but he does not bother me.

#

ANGELS

One morning, it occurred to me, if there were Spirits here, why not Angels instead. I asked God for Angels. God sent Angels right away. There were five Angels at first. Angels that came were mostly quiet. As I went about my day, I could hear them talk to each other softly. Angels are not like dead Spirits, God's Angels are positive even though Angels are in a spirit form, they are not like the dead spirits. they can make themselves any size. Some are very tall, about ten feet or taller. The spirit of the Lord has told me that some are even taller than that. Angels never talk negatively about people.

There is a female angel that is very strict, sort of like a military-type. Just by listening to how she sounded. She followed the rules of Angels. Another was more of a follower.

And another very observant one. They all have their own personalities. At first, I did not talk to them. I did not know if it was allowed to. I eventually did.

"Good morning Angels." I said. "She can hear us?" The Angel said.

"How can she hear us? Another said. They sounded surprised. "Are we allowed to talk to her?

"Yes."... Another replied. "Some can hear us."

"But she wants to talk to us." The Angels replied. "Are we allowed to? They were talking to one another.

Angels seem puzzled, usually humans do not hear them. I like Angels around, it's like being closer to God. I did not talk to spirits anymore, just Angels. Besides, David was the only spirit I really talked to. But only to yell at him to leave me alone. Now that he was an angel, it was different. I could still hear dead Spirits, I just did not talk to them at all. They tried to talk to me but I did not answer. Maybe they wanted to know why they were here. I could not speak to them. If they were angels then I would converse. Usually Angels do not ask questions about humans.

Dead spirits are always asking questions to one another, , who is that"

They do not say positive things about people. And I hear, "she lies." The most, from them.

Having Angels around was great. They were going to be with me 24/7. Angels came and went from my apartment all the time and sometimes other angels stopped by. I could hear them when they came by, they had different voices. Sometimes I could feel their presence here.

When the dead spirits were cast out and the evil spirits tied and bound. Angels were the only ones left in the apartment. That was about the time I could say that my faith was getting stronger and bigger than a mustard seed. A Holy Bible quote. Matthew 17:20 kjv

It was about ten in the morning. I was getting ready to make breakfast. I was still bothered by the annoying spirit on my back. I have tried on several occasions to try and cast it out. I thought about Fasting. Then a thought came into my head, I believe God put it there. This evil spirit had been on my back long enough. I pray and ask God.

"God of Abraham, God of Isaac and Jacob and Moses. You are the Almighty God. Creator of Heaven and Earth. You are the Alpha and Omega. Heavenly father, I need you to cast this evil spirit off my back. This right hand of mine is your hand God, and I believe this is your hand."

This was not an ordinary Spirit, it was a demon that was on my back. An old female demon and she did not want to leave. I prayed and put my hand on my back and grabbed this evil spirit.

"In the name of Jesus come out!" I demand. I prayed with authority and demanded it to come out. The demon came out. And in a second, it ran back to my back. I prayed again in Jesus' name. I reach back and grab it with my right hand.

"Demon you come out in the name of Jesus!" I demand. This is God's hand. And you demons are cast out and rebuked. By the name of Jesus." I demand.

This time, I asked God to tie and bind the demon. In Jesus name. And destroy the demon. God sent his Angel down from heaven, within less of a second, God's Warrior came down from Heaven and destroyed the demon. That demon was dead, God's warrior struck it down with his sword, at the Lord's command. Then God's warrior dragged it back to Hell. This is what I saw in my vision.

My hand was hurting in my spirit.

The demon tore up my hand. I could feel the pain in my hand like it was raw to the bone. I ask God to heal me in my spirit. God made my hand whole again. It was like a new hand and arm. I realized my back needed healing too. I do believe God put the thought in my head. To cast out this evil spirit. By demanding it come out. It had bothered me for months. It was gone. Praise the Lord thank you Jesus. Hallelujah!

#

One night, I got up to drink some water, as I was standing in front of the kitchen sink. I felt something weird on my cheeks. I was a little disturbed by it. There was something on my cheeks. It was dangling on my cheeks as I drank water. My eyes felt hollow and empty, like something missing. It was my eyes.

Even though I still could see in the natural world. In the spirit world my eyes were missing. I was a little disturbed, to say the least. But I was not going to be afraid. If I lose anything in my spirit, I will lose it in the living. I walked to the bedroom to lay down. It was obvious, I was attacked in my sleep. I did not cry, I was not going to cry. It is not that I did not want to. It's just that, crying for me, was accepting defeat. That is why I never cried. I was not going to accept defeat. And I was not going to panic. Instead, I began to pray like I always do, when I was attacked by the enemy.

I was just going to ask God to give me my eyes back. I put my music on that I always played while God was healing me. I cannot mention the title, but I will call it Jesus walking on water.

"God this is your song from me to you." I said. "I dedicated the song to you, God."

The song is how I feel about you God. How I love you God and Jesus. It is a beautiful worship song that helps me get into the presence of God. As the music played, I began to pray. As I was praying for my eyes. I then heard an Angel.

"He's coming." The angel said.

And Angel was carrying my eyes on a tray. I felt it, when God put my eyes in my sockets. It was only a matter of seconds. When God was finished putting my eyes in. I praised God and went back to sleep. I thank the Lord in the morning again. I walk to the restroom to use the toilet. I looked in the bathroom mirror and was reminded of what happened last night. As I was looking in the mirror, to see how my eyes looked, I could hear an angel arriving in my room. I could feel the Angels looking at me through the mirror. The Angels are looking at my eyes. I thought.

"How is she doing?" The Angel said.

With a strong firm voice. By his manner of speaking, I could sense he is an angel of high authority and rank. I could also sense more Angels looking at me, through the mirror. Angels are looking at my eyes. I was staring at the mirror to look at my eyes.

"She is fine." Another Angel replied. Still looking at my eyes.

"Well contact me, if you have anything to report."

He then left the room. I was getting ready to put my eye makeup on when the Angels told me not to.

"There's something in that product that is dangerous for your eyes. and you just had eye surgery." The angel said.

"Okay, but which one? I said in my mind. I was using two powdered eye makeup. She told me which one. I did not throw it away at first, probably because I paid a lot of money for it. I eventually did. So I just put on my face makeup instead. I still had a full house of angels. It was great. I only wanted Angels around, but Spirits came in the apartment somehow. I asked God to cast all the Dead spirits out of the apartment. I do not like the spirits in the home. And besides, God does not want me to talk to dead spirits.

I knew when evil spirits came around, my heart started racing. It was a danger I felt, that's what my heart was telling me. A warning that the enemy was nearby.

Evil spirits come around where a large number of dead spirits are. It's best not to have Spirits hanging around the house. I had to act fast enough, so that I did not get hurt. If the evil spirit was too huge. Then I ask God for several of his warriors to destroy the enemy. Evil spirits are in different sizes from very tiny to some to cover a house. I asked God to tie and bind the enemy and cast the demons to the street. God warriors thrust their swords at the demons and witches. The reason I ask God to cast them out to the streets. I do not want demon spirit blood in my home.

One night, I was awakened in the middle of the night. There was a smell in the room. I had smelled it before, it was Spirit blood. I was bleeding in my spirit. I had been attacked by the enemy, that devil took half my spirit body. I must have forgotten to pray before I went to sleep. It was a big evil Demon that came into my room while I was sleeping.

I woke up to half of my body, it was torn off or bitten off. I was not going to panic or cry. I did not get emotional, I just began to pray and trust in God. I looked for my laptop that was laying on my bed. I needed to put on some music, for healing. Then I laid back on my bed. And began to pray to God. I ask God for healing as I prayed, I reminded myself of all the healings God did for me.

"God, you gave me back my eyes, healed me from stab wounds and answered my prayers when I asked. This is a small task for my God. Almighty God you are great and you can do anything. You made Heaven and Earth. You are the Alpha and the Omega.

You are the creator of Heaven and Earth, God give me back my body in the spirit and in the flesh. in Jesus' name. Praise the Lord thank you Jesus." I said.

I said my prayer this way, not to remind God but to remind myself of all the wonderful things God did for me. My body in the spirit was whole again. I really do not need the christian music to have faith. It helps me stay focused.

#

WARRIORS

The Angels that God sent me are great. They are Guardians and not Warriors. And I was getting really tired of the unexpected night attacks. So, I asked God for Angel warriors. That is what I need, I thought to myself. I prayed for Angel warriors. It started with three warriors for a few nights To guard and protect me from evil. I ask God to place them on each corner of the bed. I know what you're thinking. How can this be? Angels are very tall and big. Remember, they are in another dimension. So space does not matter to them. There are no obstacles and it's supernatural. They can go right through material.

God's warriors came every evening and stayed until morning. This went on for weeks. Angels were in my room looking out for me. Before the Warriors arrived, I was badly wounded in my spirit. I had cuts and gashes on my back and stitches all over my body, from all prior attacks. The Warriors assigned to protect me, never said a word to me. I knew they were with me all night long. I can sense them here with me.

There are two other angels named Ron and Samuel who I came to depend on. They are not warriors but prayer Angels. Ron and Samuel came every night to pray for me. And asked the Holy Spirit to be placed around the house, because I asked. So basically what I am asking is for God to shield me. I do not know why but when I prayed, it was not there in the morning. They were better at it. I could count on these angels to place a shield around the house and not let evil spirits come into my room. I was not going to get hurt anymore, at night. I had Warriors and guardian angels with me at night and day. How awesome was that.

At times there were four Warrior angels in my room. Waking up to four angels, one of each corner of my bed. How can I describe it, just a blessing. I slept with only a muscle shirt , because it is summer and I was not going to change my habit. And as far as I was concerned, angels to me, are holy like the pope or nuns.

This morning, I was going to move my bed from one side of the room to the other side. I was still injured in my spirit and I was healing from my wounds from all the night attacks. But I did not let that stop me from moving my bed. I had the bed standing up right. When I heard a voice from the corner of my bed frame.

"A woman after my own heart"! The warrior shouted . In a deep voice. "He talks, Awesome."

The Warriors' voice was very beautiful. The most beautiful deep voice a man could have. It sounded medieval, like running waters. I envision him tall, then again most angels are. He was very handsome. Big structure for an angel. My thoughts were then again of my bed. I thought of asking the Warriors to help me move my bed. But I dare not ask, they are warriors not moving men. Now, the Warriors have never spoken to me, at any time they have been here. They have only coughed or cleared their throat. Except for Ron and Samuel. The regular guardian Angels have always talked to one another.

"What is your name? I asked.

"My lady, my name is Paul, at your service." He said Nice, well I need to finish moving this bed.

It seems I was sleeping too close to the kitchen vent. I did not sleep in the kitchen, rather my bed was on the side of the wall that was by the stove. Spirits came in through the vents then through the walls. Probably why I was badly injured every morning. Not that they caused it. But when too many spirits come around they almost invite evil spirits by their presence in a room.

God's warriors always left around seven in the morning. I knew I had to ask God for Paul to stay with me as a Guardian angel. Before the Warriors left this morning. I asked God for Paul the warrior. If I could keep him 24/7 as a Guardian angel. The Lord let me keep Paul as my guardian angel. I not only had angels with me, but now I had a warrior Angel with me. Awesome!

I like Paul's presence with me. And his warrior skills are a big plus for me. Paul followed me around everywhere, but only because he was assigned to me, by God. He is my Guardian warrior angel.

Paul did not talk much. He looked after me day and night. He protected me along with other Warriors. It was like that for a while. Paul followed me to work. There are many evil spirits at my job site. But just about any establishment, there are spirits there. The evil spirits came from the floor, the ceiling, through the door. They attacked me, while I was working. It was a little difficult to do my job. I said a lot of prayers when I was at my job and I'm sure Paul did a lot of fighting. In my vision and my mind, I could see a battle in the office. The battle was all around me on top of the air. God's Army of Warriors are fighting the enemy. I pray for the Holy Spirit, so that I do not get hurt.

Sometimes, I'd join in and help the Warriors, by asking God to tie and bind the evil spirits all over the office and the parking lot too. So the battle would end faster. No one in the natural world was going to get hurt. It is not something you can see. And if they did, God healed them in the spirit, through prayer. Evil spirits are everywhere on Earth. It is another dimension they carry on, almost like the natural world.

There were times, I was attacked on my face. I was cut up real bad in the supernatural. I call upon God. And God would heal me, by sending these surgeons down to work on my face. Any part of my body, God healed me. I had many of God's surgeons come down to stitch me back up but with no pain. I asked God to always heal me and to make me more beautiful in the spirit than before. Why not?

"God you are beautiful and your work is beautiful in Jesus name." Hallelujah! One evening, David flew by my side.

"They're coming!" He shouted.

"I know."

I knew I was in danger, I did not fear the enemy. As I was laying on my bed, I closed my eyes to sense things better. I prayed to God, and read the Holy Bible scripture and said, "Ask and you shall receive." In Jesus' name I ask for God the Holy Spirit around me.

Luke 11:9 kjv

"God, I need the Holy Spirit around the house. I need warriors here to fight the enemy."

God sent his Warriors down from heaven. The enemy crossed a couple of blocks radius. They must have already been nearby, before I prayed. I could see the battle, they were fighting in the sky. The clanging of swords. Demons could not cross the shield without becoming weak and then destroyed by getting too close to the Holy Spirit.

I was getting tired of concentrating, as I was laying on my bed. "Boddie, wake up!" "Wake up Boddie." David said.

Boddie was the name David had given me when he was a spirit. It was because I was human and had a skeleton with flesh. The fighting was still going on strong. I asked God for the five mile radius of the Holy Spirit. I sensed more was coming. Paul is in the room, I know he wants to join the battle. It was too much for the enemy and they started to retreat. God's angels are winning the battle. I could see God's Angels killing the enemy in the thousands with their swords outside the five mile radius. God's Warriors destroyed the demons in the sky.

There was demon blood everywhere God angels fought a glorious battle. After the battle, the area was cleansed. I asked God to cleanse it. And erase the enemy's memory of the battle that took place here, In Jesus name.

"Erase the enemy's memory of me, God.

No evil substance can be left in the ground or the enemy will try to find out who killed their own. It was over for the time being. I was tired of concentrating. I don't think anyone knows that a battle was fought here in the supernatural in a small town called Fresno, California. How did the battle become my battle? Why me? Was it because I stayed in the spirit world too long? I wanted to help God's Angels and I was not going to let the enemy take me down. At times, I felt like I was one of God's warriors.

Paul has been with me for a couple of weeks and hasn't gotten any sleep, since he has been my 24/7 Guardian Warrior Angel.

"Paul takes the night off." I said.

I know you could use some sleep. I did not know why I had not given it much thought about this matter.

"I don't need much sleep." Paul said. "I can also sleep standing up."

Sometimes another Warrior stayed here with Paul. His name is Markel but today he was out on assignment.

"Let me ask the Lord for a couple of warriors for the night, so you can sleep." I said. I have been told by the spirit of the Lord, that Angels do not need much sleep like humans. Angels can go on for weeks without sleep.

"All right then, I will come back early in the morning." He said.

When the Warriors arrive on Earth. I have to say, we're a little cocky and seem obnoxious, not what I expected. I thought who am I to question their personality?" I fell asleep, knowing that God's warriors will be protecting me throughout the night.

When I woke up, I did not feel right. As I made my way to the bathroom, I smelled blood. This was Spirit blood. When I was using the restroom, I heard the spirit of the Lord.

"Pray for yourself." The spirit of the Lord said.

My breathing was shallow and something happened in the night. "Ron, Samuel, I need you to come over." I said. in Jesus' name. Trying not to panic.

"Angels, I need prayer and your assistance." When two or more agree, it shall be done. In Jesus name. Matthew 18:19. kjv

"My lady." The Angels said.

Then they were silent, for a moment. I knew from their voice that it was not good.

"We need to pray for you." The Angels said. "We need Paul here, he needs to join us in prayer.

"Paul, come down here!" One of the Angels said. "Oh, I see." With a cracked voice, by the sound of it.

I still have my body but my spirit was lying by the closet. My spirit was cut up badly, near-death. The only reason my body was mobile was because my flesh body had not caught up to the injuries from my spirit. I do know that it would not have taken long, without prayer.

My left hand was crushed, my ribs were broken, and my foot was crushed as well. Those were some of the injuries I could feel. There might have been more, I was starting to feel it in my flesh. My spirit had taken a beating. The Angels Ron, Samuel and Paul prayed for me. We prayed for God to return my spirit back to my body.

"God heals my body, In the spirit and in the flesh." We prayed.

I could hear my left hand getting healed. It sounded like crushed bones rattling, then it stopped rattling. It hurts on a scale of one to ten, close to four. Then I heard my left foot get healed. The sound of rattling bone pieces, then it stopped. Crushed bones hurt when they are being healed in my spirit. My ribs were also broken. God healed my spirit. I cannot exist without my spirit. I was told that it takes a couple of hours for my spirit injuries to catch up to my flesh. I am only telling what I heard. My body stayed alive for hours with the help of the Angel but that is just the flesh.

"What happened to me while I slept, Angels? Then there were the Warrior angels. What happened to them?" I asked.

I thank God for healing me, And Jesus for making it possible. I thanked Angels, Ron, Samuel and Paul for praying for me. Still, how could the warrior angels just leave like that, I thought. Paul stayed the morning with me. He did not go back to Heaven right away.

Later on in the day, Paul was looking at his scroll that he looks at, to see the past. Angels also read your mind, they know everything about you before they are assigned. The Angels know my thoughts. It's hard to keep anything from Angels. They always knew what I was thinking whether it was a good thought or a bad thought. Paul flew up to heaven, he was going to find out about those three Warriors. He was not gone long, maybe a couple of hours. When he returned he told me what happened. This was what he found out.

"The three Warrior angels that were assigned to you, did not make it at all. They were intercepted by demons." The Demons took the form of the Warriors, and got into the house. " Paul said.

"They must have been nearby, when I was praying to God." I said. I thank Paul for finding out what happened. That solved the mystery of the warriors.

I was working in the office and looking forward to lunch. For my lunch break, I wanted to be alone, away from people. Besides, I wanted to talk to the angels and see how one of my friends was doing. I walked to the parking lot and stood by my car. I looked up towards heaven. David was in Heaven. I wanted to know how he was doing.

"God, I like to speak to David who is in Heaven. In Jesus name. David. David." I called out for David to hear me in Heaven.

"Boddie, Boddie is that you? He said with excitement in his voice. "Yes, it's me." I said. "I just wanted to know how you're doing up there? "How are you doing that?" He said.

"You mean talking to you from here. I believe I can, in Jesus' name. I close my eyes and look up to heaven and believe. When I close my eyes it's as if Heaven is right here with me.

I'm so happy for you. What is heaven like?" I said. "Oh... It's beautiful up here." He said.

"This is a big change for you. I do not think you realize it. You have found favor with God."

"I'm coming down." David said. In a split of a second he was in my car, along with other Angels that were with me.

"What are you doing here and what happened to your studies? I was not really expecting an answer.

I do not know if he needs to know the fundamentals of being an Angel. David did not answer me. But I did ask the spirit of the Lord about that. They don't need to read it, it's just put in their mind. I spoke to David as if he was one of my own Sons. He ignored my questions when he was on Earth or I could not hear him. He started talking to the other angels in the car.

Angels can make themselves two inches small. I know, because I hear a lot of Angels in my two seater car. I could not reach the back seat space of my car, without an angel telling me to be careful. It's just great, a blessing.

Most of the time, I talked to Angels in my mind. Especially if people are around. I cannot let them know I'm talking to Angels. There are unbelievers in the world and they will not understand. I do not care to be labeled. Just because I can hear them, it does not make me not normal. I consider myself a Christian. Some Christians can hear the spirit of the Lord and believe in the Supernatural. You have to believe in the Supernatural as a Christian . Isn't Faith Supernatural? I mean to have faith you have to believe. It's not like you can take a pill to believe, right! I hear the word of God either through God or his angels. And I'm sure some Christians experienced the same.

I can hear Angels better when they are further away. The further the better. Sometimes, when they talk directly to me, it's hard to understand what they are trying to tell me. I always tell the Angels to talk to one another so I hear you better. Only through my mind can I hear them. The Angels have a different voice from the Spirit of the Lord. Angels have childlike innocence, but are not like children; they are very intelligent. They are sweet and kind with different personalities.

Soon as David started talking to his friends in the car. He forgot about me. Outside my car, there was a spirit girl that wanted to talk to David. They spoke for a moment outside the car. He told us he had to go back to Heaven. I think the change might be a little difficult for David. The next day, when I got home from work David was there.

"Why are you here?" I said.

Go to your new home and study or something. He was there in my apartment not really wanting to talk.

"What is wrong?" I said.

It was apparent he did not want to go to Heaven. It took some time to find out what was going on.

"I cannot read." He said.

I never knew, all those times I spent reading out loud it was because he enjoyed listening to someone read. I guess in the year 1854 not everyone went to school, especially if you were raised up in secluded mountains.

"David, you will learn to read." David, we're going to pray for you that God will give you the knowledge to read any book you pick up." I said, still speaking to him through my mind.

After we both finished praying he picked up a book and began to read. The Holy Bible... Hallelujah…David flew home to Heaven. I was told by the spirit of the Lord that David could have asked God.

#

It was late in the evening, and I was feeling a bit uneasy. The night before I had gone to visit a family member at the coast. That the spirit of the Lord told me to pray for my family out there. I pray for God to watch over my entire family there.

"Paul please go and destroy the enemy at the coastal area." I said. "God, Paul will need some help." I asked.

"Markell please assist Paul."

Then I prayed to God to tie and bind the enemy at the coastal area, along the beach shore, In Jesus' name." I said. In my prayer I forgot to mention how much area needed to be cleaned up. The term clean up meant to destroy the enemy. Paul and Markell headed to the beach shore to destroy the enemy at the shoreline. I asked God if that was okay for them to both go.

Markell and Paul are very huge angels. They have known each other for many years; they have fought many battles together, I was told by Paul. Markell is approximately one thousand five hundred years old. Paul is about two thousand years old. Still in Earth years they look like they're in their twenties. Angels do not age. Paul mentioned to me that he witnessed the birth of Jesus Christ.

"There were eight Angels there to witness this event." Paul said. "How long were you there praising the newborn king?"

"A few weeks." He replied.

Paul was not only a warrior, he was also a commander. At one time, he defeated the demon named Edikar and his army of a hundred thousands. They were trying to get a hold of the city of Milpitas, by surrounding God's Army. The enemy was no match for God's five hundred thousand Angels that were with Paul. He knew the land and turned the tables around, to win the battle. As was told to me, by Paul.

"It is only written in the Book of Angels that is in Heaven." Paul said.

Markell is another mighty warrior who is modest and kind. Who also has fought many battles side by side with Paul. Markel told me he slayed many serpents, and that he once had to leave and let another warrior finish the job of killing the serpent. Because he was called to the front of the lines. He did not want to tell me the story, but I insisted. Both angels are very handsome angels. Both have broad body structures, which I can see in my vision.

When I woke up in the morning, Paul had just arrived to tell me that the work was finished on the coast.

"And this took all night?" I asked.

"My lady, we took care of a good third of the coast."

I did not realize they were going to cover that much. I should have asked the Lord for more Warriors. I could just imagine how tired they were. So I asked God to refresh the warriors and cleanse them from the residue they must have had from the killing.

Refresh was like taking a bath and drinking strong coffee but in a Heavenly way. "I feel much better."

"So do I."

They were no longer tired. Markell left. He wanted to see his friends in heaven and take care of something on Earth. He was not gone long.

"I thought you had to be somewhere?" Paul said.

"My friends on Earth do not believe I have been working." Markel replied. "What do you mean?" Paul said.

"Look at me, I have never been so clean so fast."

"I did not realize that being so clean could create a problem." I said.

Markell said his friends were so amazed that his wings were so clean and sparkling after a battle.

"Markell, do you want me to talk to your friends? I would gladly talk to them on your behalf." Markel came across to me like a sincere angel.

"Maybe. He said.

He soon flew away. He said he had some business to attend to, on Earth and in Heaven. It must have been fine after that, Markel did not return my assistance. I do not like being alone at night. The enemy never sleeps. I asked the Lord for warriors to be at my home every night. Usually about four warriors came by in the evening, including Paul before I went to bed..

The Angels guarded the apartment and my room. One warrior in the living room and three Warriors in the bedroom. They stayed until six in the morning for a couple of months, this is how it was every night before I went to bed.

I was going to church early this morning, to catch the morning service. Before getting dressed for Sunday service, I headed to the kitchen for a cup of coffee. There is a portrait of Jesus sitting on top of the microwave. I just knew it was the face of Jesus when I painted it. My kitchen was dim, as I walked towards the microwave to heat up my coffee. When I heard,

"Sire." Paul said. in a strong but respectful voice, to my painting of Jesus.

From what Paul has told me, he knew Jesus and has had many conversations with him. "He looks so real." Paul said.

I got dressed and headed off to morning service. At the parking lot church service, a lot of attendants direct us where to park. As I entered the church, I was greeted.

"Hello, glad you could join us." The church greeter said.

I sat with Paul and two other angels. Some of the angels that came with me went to stand in the back of the church. Angels are very tall and never like to sit, at least the ones that were with me. I always wondered if any church members could see the angels. I mentioned to the angels that when we enter a church, I like them to enter the church in their full Glory, wings and all. For me to identify them and not Spirits that walk the earth. I could not call Angel Spirits. I refer to them only as Angels.

The music was playing modern Christian, I always enjoyed singing along with them and praising the Lord. Hearing the word of God is always a blessing for me. After church service. We walked back to the car, I wondered how all the angels that came with me fit in my two seater car. Going from nine foot angels to two inches angels. Incredible, just incredible... Glory to God...

"Did you Angels enjoy the service?" I did not hear an answer
Talk away, but not directly at me. So that I can hear." I said.

I put the radio on and listen to some Christian music. The rest of the day went fine. I usually watched a little T.V. and snacked a lot. I have a problem with food, when I get bored I eat. But I do not try to finish what I'm snacking on. I like to munch on this and that. I was changing the channels on the set.

"If you watch horror movies, we will have to leave you." The angel said "Why?"

"Because we have too. It brings bad spirits to your home. You must not watch evil acts on TV., what's so ever." The Angels said.

The Angels were right. I do not need to watch anything evil. I ended up watching a PG animated movie instead. It was about dinner time. I decided to make enchiladas for dinner. My son was coming over and my roommate was going to be home soon. We shared a two bedroom apartment. I like cooking for others. I have not cooked that much, since I have been living alone. Don't like to cook for myself.

As I was preparing dinner, I could hear spirits in the kitchen talking to each other. This is a good time to clean the house, I thought to myself. Sometimes I asked angels to help me clean the house. Angels, we need to cast Spirits out of the house. Still talking to them in my mind. Dead Spirits attract evil spirits. I was not allowed to speak to dead spirits. The Angels prayed for all dead spirits to leave. That is how we clean the house.

There are Angels that drop in on a daily basis, and are not assigned to me. God's angels are always welcome. Angels are always a blessing, to have around me and in my home. I needed to tell the Angels a little bit about me, that was not assigned to me but we're curious about me. And they probably did not know the danger I was in or that they could be hurt because of me. I needed to give a speech to the angels that are around me. I felt it was important. Angels, I have something to say speaking to them through my mind.

"I need to remind all the angels that are with me, that you need to protect yourself. I'm not your typical human. I am almost always under attack. You must be ready to protect yourselves. And to tie and bind the enemy. I do not want you Angels to get hurt. I know you like being with me, and I like having you around. And for the new Angels not assigned to me. You need to do your homework. It is just that, at any time we may be under attack. By doing your homework, that means reading your Angel book, Holy Bible and learning everything about me. I have been under attack just about every day for almost two years. It's best to know what you are up against. I like you angels and do not want any of you hurt, because of me. You might get hurt or witness something not so pleasant. I cannot see you angels, as you know. Like I said, I do not want you to get hurt in any way. This is all new to me, I had to learn fast.

Faith, that's what kept me alive, in the spirit world. I trust in God, his son Jesus and the Holy Ghost." I said. Still talking to them in my mind.

"I have been under attack day and night, for some time now. When I am asleep, I do not know how many of you angels are going to be with me at night. Or if you will be here in the morning. I do not want anything to happen to you. I love all of you Angels. That's all." I said.

I hoped I was not out of line, but I know some of the angels are Guardians not Warriors. I never thought I was out of line, back then. God is good. I finished making the enchiladas for dinner and asked the Angels if they liked some. Paul and all the Angels ate enchiladas, not the same ones I cooked, but Heaven sent. I asked God if they taste like I cooked them. One of the reasons the Angels can not eat my food, is that there are chemicals in our food. The other is the fact the Angels will not manifest to me. The spirit of the Lord said.

I do not know why I can hear Angels and spirits so clearly. At times, it's hard to make out, if it's people or spirits talking nearby. If I am in a public place, I only talk to angels through my mind. If I am in the car, that is different. I can easily talk to them or sing out loud. Or praise the Lord out loud. I quickly learn how to survive in the spirit world. My survival book is God's word. I enjoyed talking to God's angels and asking the Angels questions.

"What is Heaven like? God's kingdom?"

"People need to be saved to enter into God's kingdom and the only way is accepting Jesus as your personal Lord and savior. Jesus the son of God, is the only way." The angel said.

"Yes, God is good."

As I was writing this, my heart started racing. The enemy is nearby. They have taken one of the Angels outside. I could hear Paul, he was outside fighting the Demons. I do not know if he is outnumbered. I began to pray for him.

"God please send more Warriors, we need help, please help. God protects your angels that are with me, with the Holy Spirit. In Jesus name." I asked.

The Warriors quickly arrived, to destroy the enemy. They fought for a few minutes. I then asked the Lord to cleanse the area. The enemy residue cannot be left behind. The Demons must not know of their dead, that were killed. Getting tired. It is about five in the morning.

#

PAUL AND THE COAST

I woke up early this morning with San Francisco in my mind. I thought I'd get an early start. I got dressed, packed a few things and told the Angels were headed out of town. I like the sea and the scenic view.

"We are going to the Pier Angels."

The Angels somehow managed to fit in my coup, on the dashboard in front of the windshield. Just about anywhere they found space. I respect the Angels by holding the door for them and opening the door long enough, as well as when they exit. I like them to feel welcome. God made Angels remarkable.

I thought I would stop for some gas, before I left town. I do not like to stop for gas, especially the gas station near my apartment. It usually has a lot of spirits there, not to mention evil ones. I thought I better ask God to make my car invisible in the spirit realm..

There was another time a few months ago that I asked God to make my car invisible in the spirit world. I did not want evil spirits to see me or the Angels in the car. I needed to pick up my mail from the last apartment that I lived in.

I remember driving up to my old apartment, and asking God to make me, my car and the Angels invisible in the spirit world. I closed the car door very softly and walked up to the apartment to get my mail not to make any noise. No living person lived there. I could hear some dead spirits talking outside the premises. I do not think they knew I was around. I quietly walked back to my car and left. In the spirit world my car is invisible to spirits.

As I drove up to the gas station, all evil spirits were gone. I went inside and got a cup of coffee. I could hear the spirits talking to each other about the people that walked in. After pumping gas into my car, I asked God to make us visible in the spirit word.

My drive to the coast was nice. There were a lot of Angels that came with me at first. But because, Angels know what I am thinking. It was not long when all the Angels left except for Paul and a young warrior Angel. After a while, I did not hear any female Angels. It was not until a couple of hours later, that I heard a female voice in my car.

She must have come in when I was pumping gas or flew in while my car was in motion. I wanted to get to know Paul.

"Who is she?" The female asked.

"I am assigned to her." Paul answered. "Assigned?"

"I am an Angel." He replied.

"And Angel? Can she hear us?" She said, "You ask a lot of questions."

I found a place to park near the Pier. As we walked along, I tried not to move my mouth to talk to Paul. I did not want to appear strange around people. I stopped to look at some of the vendors' art work. I could hear the female, she was flirting with Paul. We walked to the end of the pier.

"I'm taking off. Flying." Paul said.

I wished I could see him flying. When I close my eyes I can visualize.

"Awe this is wonderful. "He shouted.

From where he shouted at me, I knew where he was flying out at Sea. The female did not go flying. I had hoped she would leave. But here she was. This was supposed to be my alone time. I stood there and stared at the sea. From where I was standing, I could see Alcatraz and I can only imagine Paul flying out there.

I began to wonder if anyone could see Paul, flying around at sea. Nobody said anything to the fact that an angel was flying around out there. They could not see him either. Some people can see Angels, if they manifest to them. I only remember one person that ever saw the Angels. It was an elderly man at the church I went to one Sunday. After the church service was over, the angels that were sitting with me got up and headed for the door. The man looked shocked.

"Oh my." He said.

I knew he saw the Angels walking by. With his mouth wide open and holding on to his seat with one hand, as if he might fall. He was the only one that gave that reaction, when Angels walked by.

I was not sure where Paul was anymore, But he was not far from me. I am sure he can see me, out there. It is nice at the Pier, the weather was windy and cool. I enjoyed strolling along the Pier and looking at the ocean. I walked away from the end of the pier, and headed to the retail shops. I was just looking at all the wonderful things at the stores. I enjoyed looking at some of the artwork they had. Sometimes you see dancers or people performing with paint all over them. Today it was a dancer. I watch her for a moment, and walk inside the restaurant.

I bought a nice bread roll and some clam chowder. I sat at the corner of the street, while I ate my clam chowder and listened to some live music. A musician was trying out his talents with a guitar.

It got so noisy out here, so I walked to another part of the Pier. The weather was breezy and refreshing, I love how it feels on my face. It was getting late, so I headed back to my car. I did not want to pay more for parking space. That's when I heard Paul and the female walking behind me. We got in the car and drove home. I was getting hungry again. I really did not want to stop to eat. The female in the car kept saying how hungry she was too.

"Go to heaven and get some food." I said.

I did not invite her and I was not going to order food for her. The food for the Angels always came from Heaven. They once said that when I ordered food for them, it always came faster. How much faster? I really don't know.

"I forgot how to go to heaven." She said, "And besides, I lost my wings." How can an angel lose their wings? That was a new one for me.

"Paul, please take her to Heaven." I said.

He could not. Every time he tried, the female ended up in the trunk of my car. Then I prayed for her to go to heaven. Again, she would end up in the trunk of my car. I was puzzled, maybe it has to do with no wings.

After a while, I got hungry. I stopped for a burger and fries and asked God for food for the warriors that were with me. An Angel waiter came down to take the order from the Angels But when it came down to the female.

"I do not take orders from Spirits." The Waiter Angel said.

That's why she was not accepted into Heaven. God put her in her place, all right. The female Spirit got angry that she was not going to get to eat. After a short time, Paul came to the front of the car. He was getting tired of her whining.

"How could you do that to her bread?" He said. "She did not feed me." She replied.

The female Spirit pooped on my bread that I had just bought in San Francisco. I did not say a word. But I was mad. That was the first time I ever heard Spirits pooping on people's food. After that experience, I always pray for my food, and ask God to watch my food. God sends his angels down to guard my food, from Spirits that want to poop or do anything else to my food. I thank God.

As I was driving home, I felt a sharp pain on my neck. A spirit in my car stabbed me. I pray to God to tie and bind the spirit that stabbed me. It was the female Spirit, she was tied and bound by God. She was an evil spirit who stabbed me. Any Spirit who uses sharp objects on people is considered an evil spirit.

"Let me go." She shouted..

I asked God for healing of my neck. In Jesus name. Just then the evil female spirit convinced the inexperienced young warrior to release her.

I am not sure where Paul was, when all of this was going on. Whether he took off flying when we got near the reservoir or he was asleep. But for the rest of the trip, I did not talk to any of them. I did not like driving home with an evil spirit in my car. After she was tied up, what I should have added to my prayer was for God to throw her out of my car.

I finally got home and was happy to be home. This drive was not quite what I expected. As I was trying to untie my seat belt and get out of my car, I felt a sharp pain below my stomach. It was a slight pain.

The young Warrior accidentally cut me with his sword. It was not a small cut but a big gash.

"You need to be more careful with your sword, you hurt the lady." Paul said.

"We prayed for healing. This was some trip. To get hurt twice in a day. Not what you expect on a trip. But then my life in the supernatural world is anything but normal. (what I hear in the supernatural world is that most dead spirits do not know they are dead so they think they need nourishment.)

The next day, I thought about the trip and the bread I bought in San Francisco. I stared at the bread sitting on the counter. I knew it must have been covered with poop. I could hear the spirits talking. She is not going to eat that? I prayed for it and I asked God to cleanse it. I cut up the bread and ate it with spaghetti for dinner. I was not going to let good food go to waste. I always pray for my food and drink. I guess this trip taught me a lesson, to pray for my food.

#

I was seeing this guy every now and then. I only saw him once,if not twice a month. He was always working. I stopped seeing him, when I found out he was not single. At first I was sad, then I got mad, at him and then at myself.

David was still pursuing me. Even though we had an age difference. He was in his twenties, really more like one- hundred fifty years old.

About two weeks later, David proposed to me, I accepted Davis' proposal. I liked him and just did not love him. I figured I could learn to love an angel named David. One evening I got on a website for singles and started texting this guy on the internet. I did not think much of my plans to marry someone I did not care for. And then he is an Angel,I surely do not know if God permitted such a thing. I still had not read all the bible or understood it back then that well.

I remember, when he was a spirit and never gave me any space, always following me around every second of the day and never leaving my side. I felt smothered by him and found it hard to breathe. Even though I pleaded with him, to please stop following me around so much. I had told him on several occasions. Yes, I was going to tell him that it would not work out.

I was sitting on my bed, leaning against the wall, texting this guy that I found on a singles site. . The next thing I knew, David was in my room, standing on top of my bed. David was holding a sword with anger. That was the feeling I got from him standing there on top of my bed. I was horrified. He swung the sword and cut off my right arm. Within that very moment, I called on God for help.

"God take your angel David from here, in Jesus name. He is killing me." I shouted in my mind.

God's angels came down in a second and grabbed David and took him back to heaven. I was stunned or maybe more shocked. How could David do this act of evil? My arm hurt, it felt weird. I knew, if I had not asked God in a hurry. For God's intervention David would have cut me up with his sword. I was healed of course, after asking God for healing. I know it was partly my fault for accepting his proposal. I did not think I was doing anything wrong talking to a guy on the internet. That would make an Angel want to hurt me. I had no idea David would go crazy on me.

David was not allowed to come down from heaven for a while. He had not been an angel for very long, maybe a month or so. It was almost two months before he returned. He showed up in my apartment when I was putting a face foundation on. My heart started racing. It was racing but not for love, I was in danger. I did not know what he would do, so I remained calm.

"What do you want? I said. He just got close to me.

"Do not touch me, you need to go back to Heaven. You need help. Please go home."

"I know, I should have broken things off with you. I don't love you. I don't think I ever have. At least not that way."

"I'm sorry." He said. "Go home."

"He left with a broken heart."

The misunderstanding of the proposal. (When I was writing this I asked the spirit of the lord about marriage between an Angel and humans. He said it is not permitted. I think in my heart I kind of knew that.) I misunderstood what David ment. He said he only wanted a girlfriend.

#

It was late in the evening, I was laying on the bed. I could only feel sorry for myself, things were not going my way and I did not like my job. The guy I had been seeing was a disappointment. And then there was David the Angel, who went crazy on me and tried to hack me up. I was feeling bad about everything. I could not help but think about Paul the warrior. How his voice sounded so deep and beautiful. It's a deep sort of medieval, a little like the actor that played Moses but more deeper than his. Paul's voice gets even deeper than that, especially when he has flown overseas. I'm not sure if Paul is aware of the change of his voice. I do not know what he looks like, yet. or for that fact any of the Angels. Paul is in the room to guard and protect me, kind of like a bodyguard.

"Paul, would you please hold me?"

Not sure what kind of reaction I would get. And if he would. I probably would not have asked him, if I was not feeling so down in the dumps. I think he likes me though. I needed to be held tonight. Earlier in the week, when I was taking a shower. I could feel Paul staring at me. I could not help but ask him.

"Do you like what you see?" Not really speaking, rather a thought.

"My lady? He said. As if I caught him by surprise.

Paul laid down on my full-size bed, and held me all night. I really don't know how Angels conform to room size. He stayed in the spirit form, he told me he was not allowed to manifest to me. Angels can make themselves small and go through walls or just about anything. It was nice to be held. It was wonderful, the thought of being held. Even though he was in spirit form.

"I'm glad you are here with me." I said. He did not sleep at all that night. He held me all night long. He just held me, that's it. I asked him later on about holding me.

"I was a little afraid of holding you. I never held a human before." He said.

Even though Paul never manifested, I could feel Paul spirit holding me that night. He was a sweet gentleman angel.

This morning I was going to take a drive to the coast. My plans were to drive to Monterey then drive south on the 101 freeway. The Angels got in my small car and made themselves small enough. I held the door open for them.

I like taking drives to the coast, the weather is great. I also think better on the road. I never like stopping for gas. Stopping for gas for me was like breaking down at night on the wrong side of town. There are a lot of evil Spirits hanging around gas stations. I always pray before I get near one.

My prayer was that the Lord protect me and my angels. The angels that are with me are Guardians or Prayer Angels, only Paul is a Warrior. I went inside to pay and get some coffee. Paul comes across as a very social angel always talking to the spirits, as long as they were not evil.

I got my cup of coffee. And prayed again, that God will protect me and my Angels from Spirits evil doings. I walked inside to pay for the gas, I could hear them. The dead spirits are talking about pooping on people's coffee.

"It's funny to see humans drink the poop." A dead spirit said.

In the spirit world they do bad things to people in the natural world. People in the natural world do not know this. I went back to my car and began pumping gas. After pumping the gas in my car. I threw some trash in the bin. When I heard a spirit say " This is my space." The voice was coming from the trash bin. The rest of the Angels did not get out of the car when I went inside to pay. I could hear the Angels talking softly and quietly. They wanted me to hurry up, they were concerned for my safety.

"Too many evil spirits in the area." The angel said.

Gods Angels are not afraid, it's just that, they are not all made for fighting. They were only afraid for me. But if we need to battle. I'd asked God for warrior Angels to kill the evil spirits. I got back in my car and left with the angels.

After driving for a while, a car cut in front of me. He was driving too fast, maybe driving ninety miles an hour. And without thinking, I cursed.

"Oops." I said.

The Angels wanted to leave after that. I asked God to forgive me, of course. I was beginning to understand Angels. If you want to walk with God, you must be a good person, all the time.

"Love is very important." The Angel said. "I get it"

We stopped to take in some sites. Every time I pulled over to the side of the road, Paul took off flying near the coastline. I guess he doesn't like being in the car too long.

Somewhere in the drive, David flew down from Heaven and joined us. He wanted to know what we were up to. He got in my car and took the rest to drive with us. We stopped at another area site, named Big Sur. Paul took off flying.

"Paul, can I join you?" David asked. David wanted to try out his wings. They flew for a while before they returned.

"Not bad, for your first time, just try not to get your wings wet." Paul said.

The ocean had a beautiful deep blue and glossy look to it. I stopped at several places. It was breezy and sunny. The ocean view is just breathtaking.

"God you made this beautiful!" I shouted. "You shine."I was near Pfeiffer Park. When my window got stuck. I wanted to walk up the path to see the waterfall and did not want to leave the window open. I prayed to God.

"God please unstick my car window in Jesus name." As I made my turn to park the car. The window went up.

"Thank you Jesus."

As I was walking up the path, I heard the angels. "There are many bad spirits here." They said,

I prayed that they would not bother me or hurt me. Just then I heard evil spirits headed toward us. They were on our walk path.

"Paul." I said. I prayed for more warriors. "We got this." They said,

The Angels made sure they did not bother me. The view near the top is just too beautiful for words. It was picture perfect. A waterfall with glossing blue with green water running down a small cliff with an ocean below on sand and big rocks. It was worth the walk. I knew Paul and some of the Angels were flying around. I think it's wonderful that they can take in the sights that way.

"It must be great being an Angel." "It is." Was their reply.

After a few minutes, and a few stops along the beach, we walked back to my car. Paul and David took off flying some more. Paul was always nearby, about a couple of miles away. He was never too far.

I stopped at a city named Carmel and strolled along the shops. I like to look at paintings. I tried not to talk to Angels while I was walking and looking at the window displays.

Some people do not understand Christians talking to God. I do not consider myself strange, just different. Angels can travel in a matter of seconds from one place to another.

But this time, they were just enjoying the sights with me. The drive home was about the same. There was a reservoir nearby. It did not take long for Paul to fly out and enjoy the reservoir.

"Paul, are you in the car?"

"No, he is out flying." The Angels replied. He flew out of the window.

This was a fun drive, even though some dead spirits entered the car. They jumped from vehicle to vehicle or when I stopped. When this happens, I ask God to cast them out. I got home late from the drive. I put my things away and got ready for bed. I thank God for a wonderful day. David went back to heaven. I know he enjoyed being an angel. I could not be any happier for him.

When he was a spirit he dated many female Spirits. They were always looking for him at my apartment. David stopped coming around so much. He has been spending a lot of time with an angel named Athena. And from what I am told, is very beautiful and tall like all the angels. She is the Angel assigned to show him Heaven. He and Athena have been traveling to many places on Earth and in Heaven. I am glad he is enjoying being an angel.

I woke up to a small white light flying around me. The light was about less than an inch or quarter size. I wonder what it was, it was a small bright light. It kind of reminded me of a firefly but brighter and bigger. It left me with wonder, for a few moments. Could it be another Angel? I thought. Just then David flew in. I told him about the bright light flying around me. It's my new friend Athena. She's just curious about you. She wanted to know what you look like.

"Athena?" "Yes." He replied "Humm."

Me and David never really talk much. It's just that way, with us. After a few moments he left the room to talk to his Spirit friends and Angels. There were spirits and angels in my home. I kept casting out Spirits from my home. In Jesus name. After all the spirits are cast out, Angels are left in the room. Angels are always invited to my home, of course.

Angels have white bright aura around them. Spirits have yellow aura around and evil spirits have dark aura around them. Sometimes Spirits carry both yellow and black aura around them. This is what I see.

It was February, I was watching TV, when David dropped by. His spirit friends made a fuss when he entered the room. There are spirits and angels in my living room. I didn't care for dead spirits in any part of the apartment.

"He brought her flowers and bread." The angel said. "He placed them on the kitchen table and she accidentally knocked them down." I could not see flowers or the bread. I try not to pay attention to every detail in the spirit world. Only if it's a matter of life or death.

"David, you should not have brought me flowers. It's nice of you. But it's not a good idea."

He did not answer. I kind of wish I could have seen the flowers. so that I know what Heaven flowers look like. I thank David for the flowers and the bread. The Angels called the bread Mana, that he brought from heaven. Believe me. If I could have seen the bread, I would have eaten it.

Dead Spirits always just look at me and say negative things about me. I never mind angels watching me though it is a blessing for me. But dead Spirits are almost always up to no good. And if too many dead spirits are around, evil spirits like to follow them. I found that most dead spirits are into prostitution and worse. It is best to cast spirits out of all establishments that I go to. In the evening, David went home. I carry on in the natural world and do get things done.

After my normal morning of casting out spirits and reading the Holy Bible. I give thanks and praise the Lord for another good morning. I order food from heaven for my angels. A waiter Angel comes down from heaven and takes the food orders or sometimes I ask for a food buffet for the Angels.

#

One evening while I was watching T.V, my heart started racing. The Demons were nearby, I could see in my vision four or five of them coming towards me in the supernatural world.. I prayed to God to send his warriors to kill the enemy. The Demons were here to kill me. In my vision, I saw the warriors come down from heaven, ready for battle. God's Warriors killed the enemy with their swords.

I have come to understand that the All-mighty God is a powerful God. I believe God will fight my battles through the name of his Son Jesus. I believe this with all my heart. I consider myself one of God's Warriors. God has a purpose for me. I don't know if this is it. But, he has shown me the spirit world that I never knew existed. When my children come to visit, they see me close my eyes and talk to what they do not see.

"Mom, you're creeping us out." They say.

They do not understand the supernatural world, what I see in my vision or what I hear around me. I have never really told them either. I do live alone in the natural world. I have family and friends that I visit from time to time. I have my friends, the angels that reside with me. Angels are always with me and I would never have it any other way.

I was sitting on the couch, thinking about David. How wonderful things were happening to him now. I still like him as a friend and only as a friend.

David came by one morning with his friend and she wanted to meet me. Not being able to see them is not a big problem, but not being able to shake their hand is strange and surreal. I have to close my eyes to visualize them when they are here with me. I really did not care to have company today. This was my hair day. I have a hair appointment this morning and I told him that I was going to get a perm. They did not mind. Paul, Athena and David came along with me. I prayed before I entered the salon. I surely did not want to meet up with evil spirits there. I asked God to keep the evil spirits out of the salon for the duration I was there. It took a couple hours before my hair was done. I really did not like Paul seeing me with my hair undone this way. But then again he sees everything. All Angels do. I can not speak to the angels out loud. This is only done through my mind.

There are exceptions. If I am in the car alone. Of course I will talk out loud. "How are my angels?" I said in my mind.

"Fine," I said. "Almost done. "All God's Angels can read my mind and anyone else, for that matter.

After what seemed like forever. It was finally over. We walk to the sink for the girl to rinse me out. My hair was permed, it turned out fine and not too curly. I was surprised David and Athena stayed that long with me. David and Athena left, about the time my hair was done. I forget they are there with me. It takes some concentration to hear them, especially when it gets noisy. I do not play the radio often for that reason And when I'm driving, I like to hear the Angels talk to each other or to me.

When I arrived home, my son called to say he was coming over. It's always nice to have the boys visit. When my children visit I try hard to pay attention to them and not the other dimension of the supernatural. We either watch TV or get on the internet and listen to songs. Most of the time they have their own device for entertainment.

After my children went back home. I got to thinking about the spirits that are in my kitchen and always around food. This is one of the places they are always at. I always wondered why they like the kitchen so much. It's not like they can eat food.

Most Spirits do not realize they are dead. They think they are elite. Because they can see us and we cannot see them. A big lie they have been told by the enemy. I asked God to set up meals at missions. Missions are already set up all over the world by God in the supernatural. Maybe if they got free food, they would stop prostitution. I said to God.

Spirits seem to think that they need to eat. God set up the food in the missions. God answered my prayer for food, at the missions.

I figured if God does not think it is a good idea, then God would not have answered my prayer. We know they are dead spirits, that is a fact. Then there are the ones that just died and know they are dead. They are walking among the living because they did not make it to Heaven. They are the unsaved, the unbelievers. It is not enough to believe in God. But you must believe in Jesus the son of God and be saved. The dead spirits are the ones wandering the streets and cry out in the night.

I remember, there was one time a Spirit was trying to approach me. I was getting something from the trunk of the car. The Angels did not let the spirit near me. She told the Angels she wanted to know why she was not in Heaven.

"I believed in God." She said, I grew up believing in God. The Angel asked Her if she believed in Jesus. She said she did. But Jesus was not here yet. She did not believe in Jesus born of the virgin Mary the Son of God. An angel intercepted her from speaking to me any further, and told her to go to the mission for answers..

"I want to tell my family what they do not know." She shouted from a distance to me and the Angels.

I got an email for a job interview this morning. The job was in San Francisco. I needed to make arrangements with my brother to stay there for two weeks. I asked my brother if I could stay with him and his wife. He was more than happy for me to stay there with them for a couple of weeks. My brother Julio, is a very good person and always asked me for years if I was ever in San Jose to come over and stay awhile. So here I am, driving to San Jose. San Jose is very close to San Francisco. All my Angels came with me to San Jose. I don't travel without them.

When I was there, I tried to stay out of their way. He likes his coffee in the morning and he always gives his wife the first cup of coffee. It was nice to see that he puts his wife first. I wanted my brother to hear about Jesus. So I thought I would start with Christian music. I pulled out my cell phone to worship songs.

"Yola, I hear this kind of music all the time. My co-worker is a Christian and she plays this kind of music all day long. All day is too much." He said.

I like how my brother and his wife discuss things with each other. They never raise their voices at each other at any time that I see.

They have been married for many years and they still act like Newlyweds. They live in a small condo and have two children. One has already moved out. I stayed with them and slept on an air mattress in the living room. The angels also stayed with me at San Jose. They were with me in the living room of my brother's condo. Paul has been with me through all my travels. I spent my evenings talking to Angels, through my mind. I did not want my brother and his wife to hear my conversation.

My conversation with Paul was sometimes difficult. If he talks directly at me I could not make out what he is saying. I constantly have to remind him to talk away. I did enjoy Paul's company. And his presence with me.

I had a lot of Angels that stayed with me at my brother's condo. In the evening more Angels arrived. I ask God for food for my angels. The waiter Angel came down to take food orders. Sometimes a banquet of food was laid out for the angels that came in the evening. I enjoyed the Angels around me. Sometimes angels gather in front of my brother's condo outside the front lawn.

"We saw the light from the sky." The Angels said.

As they flew down to join the dinner party. There were so many angels that they projected a radiance of light for other angels to see. The more Angels came, the more food was brought down from heaven. I enjoyed ordering food from Heaven for my guests. I do believe free food was getting around with the Angels.

I think they were more curious than anything else. For that many angels that dropped in, I'd say the front lawn is a good place for them. I do not think neighbors would mind.

They can not see them anyway. Me and Paul spend time together talking through my mind. I like his presence with me and the feeling I got when he was around me.

Paul always took long walks alone in the evening. Or he'd take off flying around San Francisco. One afternoon, we all took a drive to the beach. As we walked along the shoreline of the beach. Paul told me of his War Stories and Jesus. That he witnessed the birth of christ. He was one of the eight angels that night when Jesus was born. I enjoy listening to his stories. I asked the spirit of the Lord about Jesus' birthday. Jesus' birthday is January four of the year and that the calendar was off.

It was nice waking up to Angels around me. There is an Angel named Minna who is very interesting and a pleasure to listen to. She reminds me of a maid in an old movie I once saw. The maid had a childlike innocent voice. No matter what was going on Minna got everyone's attention. And whenever she entered a room she was talking a mile a minute with her sweet voice.

"Minna, can you come in any quieter." The Angel said. "Oh, But I….Minna said. Then she went on and on. "Minna," Another Angel said.

The angels tried to keep their distance because of the air mattress that I was sleeping on. For the most part the Angels stayed on one side of the living room. But just then, Minna the Angel walked by, her feather wing tip scraped my right foot and punctured the air mattress I was sleeping on. My foot hurt from the Angel wing.

"Minna, you can't get too close." The angel said. "Oh, I am so sorry."

"It's okay." I said. "It just needs a little prayer." I enjoyed having Angels around. We prayed for my foot and God healed me. Thank you Jesus.

Once on a road trip I asked Angel Ron about earthquakes.

I soon started working as an esthetician while in San Jose. The Angels followed me to work. After two days I could not do the job required of me. I could not wax people. I was just grossed out. By the third day I did not go to work. On the fourth day I called the owner. I said I wasn't going to be able to do that kind of work. I can only look at my own body parts and not other people that close. Angels agreed, this was not the line of work for me.

"God does not want you to do this kind of work." The angel said. I needed to find another job.

#

GOD'S HAND

I answered an ad for a car salesperson and got hired right away. I was to start in a couple of days. I was going to need some clothes so I ran back to my hometown to pick up some clothes from My son's garage. I wanted to see my family too. I decided to spend two days in town to relax. What better place than my son's apartment.

My son and his roommate had plans for the evening. So I was left alone at their apartment. I pulled out my paints and put some Christian music on from my laptop. I was ready to paint ocean scenes. They are always so beautiful and some are breathtaking. I knew the Angels were around me in the room, and that was great.

"What do you think Angels? Ocean scene?" I got into my painting and after a few hours of painting I got stuck. I thought I would ask God for help.

"What do you think it needs God?" " I'm sure you know what is wrong with my painting." I could use your assistance here God in Jesus name." My painting needs something, not quite finished. I picked up the brush slowly and waited for God to paint my picture.

"It needs a little green." The spirit of the lord said. The spirit of the Lord spoke to me, what colors to use. I mix the right colors together to get the right shade of green. Though I felt, I was not really the one doing the mixing of colors. I just let God move my hand. I let the Lord speak to me in my brush strokes. I stood back, It was finished. I wanted to cry, it looked finished. I signed it and put a cross for God, next to my signature because we both painted it. I set it aside to dry and placed it on top of the kitchen table, leaning against the wall. I stood back and just stared at the painting. God had helped me paint.

Wow, how awesome is that. Praise the Lord! I cleaned up and tried to relax. Right about this time, my son and his roommate came home to their apartment.

"How's it going?"

"What are you painting? Nice. Goodnight Mom." As they walked by, heading to their own rooms.

"Goodnight boys." I did not tell the boys who helped me paint the ocean sea. I got ready to go to sleep. My night accommodation was the couch. The apartment is only a two bedroom. I stared at the painting after getting the couch ready to sleep in.

It was late in the day when I drove back to San Jose with my Angels. I needed to see about this car selling business. It was fine for a few days, working as a car salesperson. Driving new cars was great. I enjoy talking to people about everything. It was fun more than anything else.

For the next few weeks, Paul and the Angels were with me at the dealership. The lot was huge with cars and trucks. Walking around the car lot and driving the vehicles was great. I walked far away from people, so they could not hear me talk to the Angels. Once we were walking around the lot, and Paul decided to take off flying to check out the sites of San Francisco. But if I needed him for something, he was here in a second.

The Angels were standing in the dealership, or more like floating high above the ceiling. Their voices are coming from the ceiling of the building. The Angels are tall, I know they are looking down at me, while I was working.

"Paul." The Angel called out. When this young salesman walked by. "That is not Paul." Another Angel replied.

The young man mistaken for Paul has broad shoulders and is very handsome with deep blue eyes, not large but normal sized eyes and a beard with reddish brown wavy hair. He was one of the salesmen that work there. I do believe the angels had intended for me to work at this dealership. so that I can see what Paul looks like. I found myself staring at this young man. He was quite handsome indeed. So that's what Pauls looks like, I thought to myself. I tried not to stare at him. I was studying his features. I hope he does not get the wrong idea.

"Nice." I said. " He is very handsome."

I was still learning the business and did a lot of talking to customers but selling vehicles was not that easy.

It was hard not to look at Paul's look-alike. Since the Angels made it a point that this young man looked like Paul.

"Angels, you knew there was a look alike at this dealership," I said. "Angels, how could you get me in this situation?" Speaking to Angels through my mind.

I could not get mad at the Angels, at least I knew. I have been here three weeks and still have not sold a single car. God does not want me to work at this dealership, that was obvious.

I was sitting down at the break room eating my lunch. I tried not to pay too much attention to what was being said. Just then I heard new voices. These voices were deep. Strong voices are sort of medieval, just like Paul's voice. Their voices definitely reminded me of Viking warriors in movies. They came to the dealership looking for Paul.

"Where is Paul? The Angel said. "Paul!" Another shouted.

It was not long when Paul heard their voices that he was here. I always wonder how they do that. Make themselves small enough to fit anywhere, but I guess it's because Angels are in spirit form. And there are no barriers for them. They seem a normal Angel height.

Now this is going to be interesting. I thought to myself. To hear these Angels with Medieval voices talking with Paul. I knew they were not evil spirits.

"Paul, come, join us." The Angel said. In a deep voice. "It's good to see you." Paul said. In a friendly tone. "Come with us." Another Angel said.

By the way they were greeting each other, they sounded like they were old friends. Paul's Warrior friends came by to take Paul with them. They were going out to Sea this morning. It was so remarkable to hear their voices. I feel truly blessed to hear warriors talking. This was my first time hearing other Warrior voices. Except for Markell and Paul, When they had to take care of the coast.

I can say now that I heard Warriors talking to each other. Most of the time when they were with me, they were assigned by God. They were on duty that's probably why they never spoke. It was nice to hear them. They were planning to spend some time out at Sea and do some fishing.

"Paul, go with your friends." I said, speaking to him through my mind.

"Everything will be fine." He needed convincing, by his comrades. I don't know if it was me or the angels that convinced Paul to go with his friends.

"If anything happens, just call out to me. I will be here" Paul said. Paul is still my Guardian Angel.

I stepped outside the car lot. It was nothing out of the ordinary, just Spirits hanging around the lot. There's always spirits around, sometimes evil ones. The Angels thought it was dangerous for me to walk the lot. I could hear Paul's voice up in the sky. As he was flying towards me. He was returning in a hurry. One of the Angels had called him. In my mind I saw him flying towards me as his voice got closer. He had only been gone for two hours.

"What's wrong?" "Paul shouted.

"Paulie, What are you doing here? I said.

"The Angels called me. Is everything alright?" He Asked.

"Everything is fine. Please go back to your friends and enjoy yourself." I said.

Paul went back to the ship. I wanted him to spend some time with his friends and not feel smothered. I wanted him to feel he could do things with his friends. And do his job of watching me. I was still getting to know the Angels and how to talk to them through my mind.

We walked the car lot and spoke to the Angels through my mind. "Angels, I want you to walk in your full Glory." Wings and all."

Paul returned after two days out at Sea. "I cannot stay away, when you might need me,"Paul said. Paul was sent here to keep me safe. He'd fight the evil spirits that wanted to hurt me.

At night, Paul takes off flying around San Francisco. After a few weeks at the dealership, I was fired. I had not sold a single vehicle. I think it had to do with Paul's look-alike. Within a week, I was hired at another car dealership. I went to work right away. I moved out of my brother's condo and rented a room. I had stayed long enough at my brother's place. San Francisco is pretty and smells like the Sea. When it gets breezy it comes in fast. Living in San Jose is nice but the commute to San Francisco can be stressful. I do not think I can get used to driving every morning in the manual car, constantly shifting gears in slow moving traffic. It gets very hard on my foot.

The room I rented was nice, but the walls must have been made out of onion skin. I could hear the tenant in the next room. My room is small, eight by ten feet, the Angels had to stay outside the room. I asked God to place a room for my angels outside the backyard.

And to camouflage the quarters for them. I do not want the angels to get hurt in my room being so small. No telling what could happen to them if they stayed small all night long.

One evening I heard the Angels talking about an army of evil spirits coming from one end of town. It was a small army of thousands that were in battle. The evil spirits were trying to take over the Bay area. What side of the city I do not know? Paul, Thomas and some of his warrior companions were headed out to fight. Paul gave instructions to the Angels to take care of things while he was away. And by his voice he sounded a little worried. The fighting was supernatural between God's Angels and Demons. This was not the big battle to come in the future. Paul was going to make sure that they were not coming towards me. I could hear the Angels around me and the dead spirits too.

The night seemed long waiting for Paul to return. I did not fear for myself but the Angels. I was very fond of my Angel friends.

Paul and all the Angels came late in the morning about 4am. He said everything was fine and not to worry. I do not recall every word said. After speaking to me of what happened he joined his Angel friends outside. Angels would leave and return from Heaven at any time. They chose to stay with me and deal with whatever I was facing.

One night, I was awakened by David. I actually saw David for just a few seconds. "David." I said.

At that moment, when I was awakened, I was able to see the angel for just seconds. He put something in the back of my knee, where it bends. It hurt real bad, Not just in my spirit but in my flesh. I had to pray fast, David was trying to disable my leg. David was not going to quit. He still wanted me, even though he knew, I did not love him that way.

He must have gotten ahold of some kind of evil witchcraft from somewhere. David had not been an angel that long. How could he not realize you cannot be good and evil. I began to pray for God to help me. I asked God for a big prayer request.

"God help me with David." I prayed. I saw in my vision God's angels come down to take David back to Heaven. I knew this was not going to stop. So I asked God.

"Erase David's memory of me." I said.

This is the only way he was going to stop from bothering me. God answered my prayers. He is still in heaven and God let him keep his wings. I don't know if God punished David. I'll leave that topic alone. The angels and I prayed for my leg. The evil stuff that was placed in the back of my knee was cast out, to the pits of Hell. In Jesus name. Then we ask for healing. My knee was better after prayer. I try not to think of all the bad stuff that happens to me. That is not good for the mind. I just live day by day in faith, knowing God is with me. I do not feel sorry for myself and I do not fear evil. 2 Timothy 1:7

I remember years back, when I had gotten into an argument with this man, it was bad. My thoughts were bad and I went to bed mad as I slept on the couch I felt something over me. I opened my eyes and I saw something dark and scary looking at me, it was something evil. I closed my eyes and I prayed to God. I asked God that I never want to fear anything evil again. And for God to forgive me of my sins.

After that experience I never go to bed mad anymore. It's been almost two years now and God has kept me alive in the spirit world. My faith is growing strong. Oh about David he is still one of Gods' Angels.

#

THE TOWER OF SAN FRANCISCO

I was still working in San Jose. I like the weather and I needed a job. After a few days working at the new job. I sold my first car. I was so happy. The Angels went with me every morning to the car lot. By the afternoon more Angels arrived, at first it was four maybe five angels on top of the tower.

The car dealership that I worked for has this tall tower billboard structure where the Angels stood every morning. I like having them around, so I asked God to send them some breakfast. And to make it comfortable up there on the tower with the canopy and some seating for the Angels. I tried to make it comfortable for all the angels everyday. I did everything for God's Angels, I love them. I made sure they got three meals a day. I did not have too, I wanted too. I could hear them talking every day up in the tower. Not long conversations, just short ones.

One time, the Angels on top of the tower wanted Paul to do something. Paul did not want to, so the Angels chased Paul around the sky on top of the car lot and through the outside of the vehicles. I could hear them laughing as they flew through and around the cars.

"No. Nooo... leave me alone." Paul was laughing as he was telling them no.

They chased him for a while, high above the parking lot too. I really don't know what it was about, but it was fun hearing them. I don't know if the Angels caught Paul, It was nice to hear him laugh though. I always walked away from other sales people. I did not want them to hear me talking to Angels. That might get me fired.

I looked up at Heaven, then closed my eyes and kept quiet. This was the best way to hear Angels. I sold a few more cars that month. I guess I just wanted to know if I could sell cars. While still working in San Francisco, I applied for a job in Los Angeles and got an interview right away. On my two days off I drove to Los Angeles. As I was driving to L.A., I began to wonder why I did not have a sale for the big holiday weekend. I asked the angels to help me sell a car for that weekend, but I had no sale.

The new girl that just started, sold six vehicles that weekend. Not even the top salesperson that had worked that weekend, sold that many.

"Angels, how is it possible that the new girl sold that many cars? I asked you angels for help, how is it, I did not sell one that weekend?"

"I did not know what you look like." One of the Angels replied.

"What I look like! Really?" I said. The Angels gave the sales to the new girl to make me feel bad, at least that is what I thought. I did not know what else to think.

"But why?

I began to cry, yes, I was crying. God said it was okay to cry. I was pouring out tears. I have not cried like this for a long time. I have been holding it in, for so long. Afterwards, I was all cried out. I got mad.

"I did a lot of nice things for you Angels." I said.

Feeling sorry for myself. Then the spirit of the Lord said to me,

"It's not the angels that did this. But an evil spirit who posed as an Angel. The evil spirit made the Angels think she was an Angel and made them do that."

Evil spirits can make themselves look like angels and can fly but are demons or witches. I need to apologize to the Milpitas Angels. I too was fooled by a Demon, passing as Angel. I am still learning more and more in the Supernatural world.

After landing the job in L. A. I started looking for a room to rent. I answered an ad for a room on the internet. I was determined to find a room. It was late July and it was hot and humid. I could not stand the weather change in L.A. I bought an air mattress for my room and moved in immediately. I did not like the area, It was so hot and crowded with people.

One night I was laying in my bed, when a snake came into my room, it was a spirit Snake. It came out of the couch that was in the living room. I never liked that couch. I always got a bad feeling from that couch when I walked by it. Where they got it from, I do not know? Some things just need prayer before it is brought inside the home. Spirits get into your stuff and they come right into your home. Another night an evil spirit woke me up in the middle of the night.

A spirit was trying to take me as a prisoner. They were chains on my palms and ropes all around my body and my face. I could feel the ropes very tight around me. The ropes had no space between them and my palms hurt badly from the holes he made with metal chains and nails . I could not move, they were so tight on my face, and my body. I did not panic, I prayed to the Lord to break these chains and disintegrate the ropes. Then I asked the Lord to tie and bind the evil spirit who did this to me. God answered my prayer.

The Dead Spirit was put out on the street. That was his punishment. He told the Angels he was looking for his wife. I do not think he knew he was talking to Angels. These are some of the wicked things Spirits do in the spirit world. I did hear him say,

"Let me go. Let me go" to a dead female spirit who took him as a slave all tied up.

The Angels around me are not warriors. When I do not hear them I get a little concerned that they might have gotten hurt. Not sure where they were, when I was attacked I must have forgotten to pray before I went to sleep. I will deal with it when I wake up in the morning. As long as I pray before I go to sleep. I know God will protect me. I have my faith that's what keeps me alive in the spirit world.

#

One evening I was looking at the internet, I wanted the Holy Bible to be read to me. I was relaxing at home and looking at the internet on my cell phone.

The Angels wanted to see what I was looking at even though they did not say so.

"Please make the screen big, the size of the room. I want my friends to see what I was looking at. I prayed to God."

The internet for me was becoming a handy tool. There were many times we looked for angel sightings. They tell me if it is an angel or fake. After a short time of scrolling through the internet. I ran across the Quran book. I had heard about it but did not know about it. I did not see any harm and opened the book. As soon as I opened the first page of the book, it was in another language.

"Close the book immediately!" The Angels shouted.

I did what I was told, by the Angels. I immediately closed the book and felt I did something wrong. I guess the Angels did not think I was going to open it.

"It will only confuse you." The Angel said. I did as I was told and did not read it. I found the KJV Bible and fell asleep listening to it.

I was working full-time hours and not spending any money so I managed to save and buy an old van. The van I wanted was twenty years old. My car was too small. I found three people that were selling their vans. There was one in Bakersfield. I wanted to see that one. It sounded good, the price was right but the spirit of the Lord told me not to go see that one.

The next one was in Santa Paula so I went to see it. I bought it, after speaking to God about it. I bought the van from a young man. He wanted a little more than I wanted to pay for and had on hand. So we negotiated that I would pay him the rest in a week. He let me take the van. And I did pay him the rest of the money I owed him, at the end of the week.

One morning as I was driving out to the coast. Paul saw an evil spirit, so he jumped out of my van unto top of the hood then drew his sword to fight the demon. Paul at one point punctured my radiator with his sword. As I was driving up to the gas station, my van leaked all the water out. There was a trail of water up to the gas station. I let my van cool down for an hour. I wasn't sure if it was drivable. I opened the hood of the van to put coolant in, which I bought at the gas station. To my surprise, it had water in the radiator.

"Thank you Lord." I said.

We drove to the beach. And spent the rest of the day there. A couple of weeks later, I drove from L.A. to Fresno in four hours. I wanted to visit my family and friends. I wanted my son to check out the brakes of my van.

When my son Jacob was twelve, he liked to take things apart. He took apart the telephone, the radio, and I think even an old TV. He wanted to see how everything worked. He likes working on cars in his spare time. I have mentioned to him that maybe this is what he should be doing as a career, since he likes it so much. I drove up to his place. And almost immediately, he started looking at the van. My son opened the hood to check things out.

"Son, I need you to look at the brakes on this van." I said.

"That is not your biggest problem, mother. Your hose on your van has a one inch cut in the shape of a y." He said. I have been driving the van for more than two weeks before I could come by.

"How is it you're driving the van with a busted hose?" He said.

My son fixed the radiator hose instead of working on the brakes that day. I spent the rest of the day visiting the family in town before I drove back to L.A.

This morning I drove this beautiful winding road with beautiful mansions on each side to the top of a hill. It was the nicest part of L. A. I was to check on a friend. On my drive up I heard the Angels talking to each other how the mansions look like the ones in Heaven but the ones here were smaller. I thought how fascinating it was to hear that.

The home had a big beautiful window to see all the way down the mountain and was so breathtaking. They had built this home because of the view. He was dying of old age and cancer. I wanted to see if he needed any help. There were get well cards on the desk, from friends and family. He asked if he could eat, so I helped him with that. I tried to spoon feed him what he was supposed to eat. Then I helped by changing his bed sheets. The Angels told me to wear gloves and not get too close to him. I was still learning the word. That must be the reason the Angel said.

"He has cancer. And it's contagious." The Angels said.

"I thought cancer wasn't contagious." Speaking to them through my mind. "This type of cancer is." The Angel said.

"There is a comforter on the floor and it is contaminated. Put on some gloves before handling it." The Angels said.

"What about the other sheets and blankets he has on his bed?" I asked in my mind.

"As long as they are washed they are fine. Wash your hands with cold water, not hot." The Angels said. I also washed the kitchen counters.

"I always thought cancer was not contagious?" I said.

"There are all types of cancer. This one is." The Angels said. I wore gloves the whole time I was there. Before I left, I asked if I could pray for him. He agreed.

#

THOMAS AND THE PARK

I drove to this campground that was at the beach shore to use the restroom. While I was in the restroom, I heard a familiar voice. It was Thomas the spirit, Paul's friend. Paul sometimes brought Thomas, when he came to see me. Paul and Thomas would jump in the van while the vehicle was in motion. He has known Thomas for many years and has fought many battles alongside Paul and all Angel warriors for hundreds of years.

"I know this lady." He said.

He was talking to a dead female spirit. I wanted to talk to him, but God told me not to talk to dead spirits. I finished my business in the toilet and walked back to the van. I looked up to heaven and prayed to God that I may speak to Paul, in Jesus name.

"Paulie," I said, "Paulie, this is me., I need to speak to you." "Yes my lady." He said. His voice came from Heaven. "Your friend Thomas is here at the beach."

Paul got here in an instant and greeted Thomas. We all got in the van and drove to another Beach. Only because it's hard to talk to them with so many people around. Normally I do not let Spirits in my van, but I made an exception for Thomas.

Somewhere in the conversation it was brought up. Of becoming an Angel.

"Why do you not ask God for wings Thomas? My lady wants to know." Paul said. "I do not think I'm worthy to receive Wings." Thomas replied.

"You wings." His girlfriend replied, with a sarcastic voice.

"Ask him, if he can do the Lord's work, at the missions, Paulie? It might help, and remind the Lord that you Thomas helped his Angels. By fighting the enemy." I said.

Thomas said, he thought about it. After a short while, Thomas and his girlfriend left. Paul went back to Heaven; he did not come down to Earth much.

It was about five in the morning, when I drove to the gym. Like any establishment I went to, I had to deal with annoying dead spirits as well evil ones. I prayed before I walked in, for God to cast all the dead Spirits out of the gym, and tie and bind the evil ones. In Jesus name.

Dead Spirits ask too many questions and are negative, about every human in the natural world. Ever since Paul has been assigned to me he has been hit-on by dead female spirits, some are witches and some are demons . They try to distract Paul, so that I do not have angels to protect me. They disguise themselves so they do not look like witches or demons. I ask God to help me. God sends his warriors down to Earth.

Sometimes it's hard to get a work out, with dead spirits around the gym, just talking all the time and trying to do nasties. They can get mischievous and do nasty things to people and me while I'm working out. I cast out spirits about five hundred feet away from the gym. In the Lord's name. At least for the time being. They will stay away from here. As I was walking back to the car with Paul and some of the Angel warriors who were escorting me back to my car. All of the sudden, I heard a voice coming from the sky. The voice was getting closer and closer toward us.

"Hello there. Still his voice is coming from the sky." "Thomas? Paul said.

Their voices sounded so happy with laughter." "Well, look at you."

"Yes, I got my wings. Sounding so excited. "They're wonderful, aren't they? I asked God for them." Thomas said. I could not see Thomas, but I could hear everything around me and visualize them.

"Thomas, that's wonderful." Paul said.

"There's only one thing." Thomas paused for a few seconds. "My girlfriend, she doesn't like my wings. She left me." Sounding a little sad for just a moment. "But, I got wings." Thomas said. I stood there awhile with the Angels, listening to their conversation about wings and flight.

"We are so happy for you Thomas. You are well deserving of wings. After a short time, I thought it was best to leave.

"Congratulations, but I have to go." I said.

I did not have to be anywhere this early, I just did not want cameras on me. This parking lot has lots of cameras. I might have taken too long standing there near my car, talking to the Angels in my mind. The Angels got in my convertible, as I started to drive away. Paul jumped in from the soft top of my convertible while my car was in motion. Praise the Lord!

One day after work I drove to the park, parked next to some old trees and sat there. I was looking at the mountains and watching people strolling along with their dogs. It wasn't long before I heard spirits nearby.

"I think she's a spiritualist." A spirit said.

"Let's ask her, maybe she can help us." Another dead spirit said.

I hope they are referring to the fact that I can hear the supernatural world, I thought to myself. I do not refer to myself as a spiritualist. It wasn't long when Paul jumped out of the van toward the trees to speak to them. The spirits were trying to talk to him, Paul was not afraid of any spirits. I think Paul is a very social Angel, he always jumps out of the car to talk to spirits, whenever I make a stop. The rest of the Angels that were with me did not come out of the vehicle. It is not that they are afraid. Angels are only interested in the living, and do not care to talk to dead spirits.

"Can she help us?" A Dead spirit asked. "What happened to you?" Paul asked them,

"A witch put us on these trees, many years ago" The spirit said. "Can she help us?" They asked again.

"I shall see." Paul replied, with a deep voice.

The spirits were hanging on the tree like ornaments. They did not say what the witch used them for. Paul did not have to tell me what they said. I could hear everything. I do not know if God would approve of me praying for them but, I figured, God will not answer my prayer if it is not right. My prayer went like this:

"God there are dead spirits hanging on trees. If it be your will and your will alone, release the spirits from the trees. In Jesus name. And tie and bind the witches that put them there. Blindfold witches and cast them out to the streets. In Jesus name." I prayed to the All-mighty God.

Witches need to be blindfolded, or they might put Dead Spirits in a trance and make the Dead Spirits release the witches that are tied up. I saw in my vision the Gods Warriors came down from Heaven and killed the witches with their swords. I then prayed to God to cleanse the area where they were killed.

After a short time at the Park, I got hungry and took out my lunch to eat. And the Angels called out to heaven for lunch. After lunch, I reclined the seat of the car and took a short nap. And prayed for God to protect me while I took a nap. It was late in the day, when we left the park.

#

RON, SAMUEL AND HEAVEN CITIZENS

It gets uncomfortable in Los Angeles. The place I lived at is hot and humid and hardly ever gets a breeze. I felt in my spirit that God did not like me living here. Something about the place I was living at was not right with the Lord. When I rented this room I did not consult the spirit of the Lord. I did not hear God all the time back then. It wasn't until I wrote this biography, that I could hear the Spirit of the Lord all the time. And ask God questions.

Good thing I purchased a van. It was more comfortable than my little car. Especially when I get sleepy, I don't have to drive for miles just to get home to sleep. It was late summer and they were recreational vehicles everywhere all summer long. I spend all my spare time at the coast. I am still working and thought I would get a second job. I took my laptop to the coffee shop and browsed . After a couple of weeks I found a job at a retail store. Good thing, my first job slowed down. so I spent more time at the store. It was hard work stocking merchandise for the holidays.

At first, I liked looking at all the new clothes that came in the store. Something about opening boxes and looking at new womens clothes was exciting for me as if the clothes were for me. The job was fast paced. And I was not fast enough. I eventually quit. I called my old job to see if they needed any help. She said they did need help and will call me back during the week.

It is late summer now and there's recreational vehicles out at the coast. I still had a job with the agency, just not full time work.

Looking out the window of my van. I stared at the coastal waves. It's just beautiful out here. I can see why everybody wants to be out here. The air feels cool and breezy. It is not always overcast and sometimes there is sunshine. It's just great. There's always great parking alongside the coast and no one usually bothers you. I felt safe out there, but then again. I relied on God to keep me safe.

It was early in the day when I drove to pick a few items from the local grocery. As I was shopping at the store, all of a sudden, I heard The Spirit of the Lord tell me that a citizen from Heaven wanted to speak to me.

"It is your son." The Spirit of the Lord said.

Is this the son I did not give full birth term, I thought. Thinking back in time when I was having problems with this man. He did not want children and he was a very difficult man to be with and of course I got pregnant. He said. "No kids," I was not happy that he did not want kids. I cried a lot and tried to talk to God. But I wasn't living right, doing worldly things. I was very confused, without a steady job. I know I did a terrible thing. I aborted and felt ashamed, like something died in me. I was never going to do that again.

I could see the young man walking towards me in a vision. He did not have a shoulder. I could see this in my vision. He looked young like the age of my other children. I did not know that babies still grow up in heaven. He then spoke to me.

"I just wanted to meet you. I do not hold anything against you. I just wanted to know who you are?" He said.

"I'm so sorry, forgive me." I said. Holding back tears. I was stunned, and could not ask him questions because I had a lump in my throat. After a few moments with him he turned and looked like he was walking away.

"Can I pray for you?" I said. "Sure."

We both prayed, but in my prayer I asked God to restore his arm and shoulder. I didn't know if I could, but I did anyway. in Jesus' name. God answered my prayer. I could see in my mind in my vision that my son got his arm and shoulder back. Right there at the grocery store. Thank you Jesus.

"Thanks. I got used to using one arm." He said.

We are so happy. I broke down and cried of course. And then he hugged me in my spirit. I just stood there frozen for who knows how long. I saw him walk back to the light.

The thought of what just happened in the grocery store. I asked God that I would like to speak to my son again. I was still a little shook up. Because this was my son and I felt horrible for my actions when I learned I was pregnant. I know God forgave me for my sins. Still I felt terrible. I'm so grateful that I have a loving and forgiving God.

Meeting up with my son was a little overwhelming, I didn't know I could talk to humans in Heaven unless they were Angels. I was going to think about this some more in the future. But for now, there were groceries to pick up. After shopping for a few things I spent the rest of the day at the beach. Thanking the lord for restoring my son's arm and shoulder.

I did not have to be at work until the afternoon, so I drove back to the park to spend the morning in a nice quiet area. I bought some fast food and took it to the park to eat.

My thoughts were about the grocery store and meeting my son. And of the spirits hanging on trees. It was a lot to think about. But I learn something and that is not to try to think too hard about anything that has happened. At least not yet.

The dead spirits that asked to be released from the trees that the witches had put them. Paul hardly ever mentions to spirits that he is an angel. Dead Spirit can not tell if they are speaking to Angels.

I gave it some thought but not a whole lot. It was about three forty-five in the afternoon,when the Angels and I were sitting in my van enjoying our lunch. When I heard voices at a distance. They sounded like it was coming from over the mountain.

"Billy, Billy wait. Maybe those people have some water?" A woman's voice said.

"I will ask them if they have some food." Another voice said. The voices were getting closer to my van.

"They are Dead spirits," The Angel said.

"Do you have water?" The Spirit asks. I do not think she was talking to me. "By the tree over there near the restroom." The Angels replied.

"I do not want them near my van." I said. At that moment I pray to God to give them some water and food. In the Lord's name.

"There are sandwiches in the basket over by the tree." The Angel said. They did not know it was from God.

"We have been walking for days without water." One of the spirits said.

The Angel said. "They are the spirits from people that died, from those mountains up there. They got lost and ran out of water."

"They found a stream that was poisoned."They will repeat this every day at the same time, until their bodies are found."

"How long have they been dead?" I asked

"About fifty years." The Angels replied. We prayed for the spirits and left the park. I needed to get ready for work. I still visit the park but not at three-forty five in the afternoon.

#

One evening I went to the store to pick up a few things and was feeling a little tired after shopping. My intentions were to head back to the beach but was getting late. I really did not feel like heading back anywhere. I asked my friends to come down from Heaven, who happen to be Angels.

"Ron and Samuel, can you watch me while I take a nap? I know I probably should not sleep in my van at a parking lot but I did not see any harm in it. Besides, I do not want to drive sleepy. And I do not want Spirits bothering me while taking a nap.

"Yes of course, my lady. The Angels replied.

It was early in the morning, when I woke up to a bad aroma. What is that smell? I thought. It smells like spirit blood. I have smelled this odor many times before.

"Ron! Ron! Samuel! Samuel!"

No answer. I felt weird, I better not move. I looked out the window , and began to pray. It did not feel right. I asked God for healing for my entire body. God I need healing in my spirit and in the flesh. As God was healing me, I saw in a vision the enemy was close by. They were still here. I was barely alive. My Angels were slain.

"God disintegrates the enemy that is in the van and outside my van. In Jesus name. Cast out all evil spirits out of the van. In Jesus name." I prayed.

"God heal Ron and Samuel, your angels, heal your Angels bodies and return their angel spirit back to their Angel bodies. I prayed. With a little emotion in my voice.

God was also healing my spirit as I was speaking to the Lord through my mind. The fact that two of God's best Angels were attacked, at the same time is a very bad thing. The Demons must have attacked us at night. They must have been in the hundreds and overpowered the few angels that were with me.

"We never saw them coming." Ron said.

My few Angels were outnumbered. This was going to be the last time that my two Healing Angels would be here at the same time, guarding me. I could not take that chance again. Ron and Samuel are not warriors, they are Prayer Guardians Angels. Paul was outside, he was not hurt but something was wrong with Paul, he did not make any sense. We're not sure what happened to him that night. We prayed for Paul. Then he flew up to heaven. Not sure what happened to him. But I knew he was going to be just fine. I do not dwell on it on all the bad things that happen to me. I just keep trusting in the Lord.

It was early in the morning. So I picked up some breakfast at a local fast food. I decided I was going to spend the morning here at the beach. I sat at the parking lot in my van and waited for an hour before I could go back to the beach. It is open at a certain hour in the morning. And I didn't have to work. The beach was becoming like a home to me. It was cold and breezy and there was no fog this morning. I parked the van facing the opposite direction and just sat there for a while. What can I say? I just love it here. I pulled out my bible to read.

Driving this evening from Santa Barbara to Ventura on the 101 freeway was cool and breezy. The weather here never disappoints me. I was thinking of my son in Heaven, and how God gave him his arm and shoulder back. Then it occurred to me, there are babies without limbs, from all over the world that died through abortion. Could they be in heaven without limbs too? I thought. It saddens me. Then I got a wonderful Idea.

"Angels, we are going to pray for the babies in Heaven that do not have limbs." I said.

The Angels and I began to pray. The Lord's prayer. Almighty God, creator of heaven and earth, I pray that you give back all babies, children and young adults that are in heaven that have grown up in Heaven. And were aborted, I pray that you restore their limbs and any part of their bodies restore them. We pray to you to give them back all their body parts. In Jesus name Amen. Thank you Jesus for making things possible. Praise God.``

We then glorify God. Glory to God in the highest hallelujah, hallelujah, hallelujah, praise the Lord. Thank you Jesus. I shouted. I could hear them in heaven. As I drove northbound on the 101 freeway with my angels. Some of them had just woken up. Even though it was about seven in the evening.

"Look." A Heaven citizen said.

"The Lord healed me." Another said.

I heard so much excitement in heaven. Paul had mentioned to me that Angels do not sleep that much. It felt wonderful that I could help in some way. I rolled down the car window.

"Thank you Jesus." I shouted.

It must have been about two weeks later that I drove the same Coastal freeway. It was late in the evening. I open my car and my window to catch the evening breeze. It smelled like the sea. Just then I thought I heard something.

"Do you hear that? I hear singing outside."

We were not near any cities. It was just a freeway and ocean. It sounds like it's coming from Heaven.

"Yes, they're singing to you." The Angels said. "The children? It is so beautiful."

I felt like crying, it was so beautiful the children were singing to me. Oh how wonderful. I felt truly blessed. I kept the window rolled down for the duration of my drive. I was praying for a good long time. I was filled with so much emotion for all the children in heaven. The singing went on for about twenty minutes. Weeks later, I thought I would pray again, for the new children that arrived in Heaven. Hallelujah

#

One morning, I stopped to get breakfast at a fast food restaurant. As I was trying to enjoy my meal, I was being annoyed by evil spirits. They were hitting me on the head as I was trying to eat my meal. My reaction was slow, I did feel some pain. I said the usual prayer in my mind, for God to tie and bind the enemies and cast all evil spirits or demons to the street. In Jesus name. After they were cast into the streets. God's Angels come down to destroy them.

The whole time this is going on, an angel is observing me from across the room I saw in a vision and sensed his presence here. It was not any of the angels that were traveling with me. It was another big angel and he was just staring at me. I got up to leave and threw the trash in the bin. The Angel that was watching me was now standing near me.

"You're amazing. I know you can hear me." He said.

I did not answer him right away. Mainly because I was in a fast food restaurant. "Who are you?" Speaking to him in my mind.

"I am an angel."

"Are you traveling somewhere?"

"Well, yes we are seeing the sights," I said. I walked outside toward the van.

"I like to go with you. I see you have a lot of Angels with you. And well, I was hoping you could also pray for me. I lost my wings." The Angel said.

I do not believe every spirit that claims to be an angel, and has lost their wings. Not all that claim to be Angels are Angels, but he sounded sincere. He followed me outside.

My name is Bartholomew and I would like to go with you." He said.

"You have to ask Paul."I wanted Paul's feedback on the matter of an angel coming with us that does not have wings.

"He has to give you the okay. And about the wings? That's up to God."

We all prayed for Bartholomew to get his wings, If it's God's will. In an instant he got his wings. He was so excited that he flew around the parking lot for a few minutes.. He got in the van after that and said he wanted to experience our adventures. Bartholomew was part of our Angel group from then on.

This morning I wanted to pick up some pants at the thrift store and possibly go to my storage unit that I have here at the coast. I never liked storage places. They have more spirits than usual. I always hear them when I go and pick up my stuff. Believe me, I do my share of praying when I am there. And this morning was no exception. I tried to be quiet when I walked down the cold hallways. I walked inside the elevator to my storage unit when I heard an evil spirit in the elevator. I stepped to one side where the voice was not coming from. And began to pray to the Lord. The Angel came down and thrust the sword at the demon spirit in the elevator. I was never afraid, I guess I am getting used to this stuff in the supernatural world.

#

THE DRIVE HOME

Paul and all the Angels traveling with me were supposed to look for an apartment for me in Santa Maria. The Lord told us to look for one the next morning. Just before we were going to do that, an Angel told us that my son was in trouble. Being it was family, I drove home that same evening. It was going to be a four or five hour drive to the valley. During the whole drive I was praying for my son's safety. I did not know what kind of danger he was in, but I needed to go home and see if everything was alright. As I was driving home that night, I felt that there was darkness in the van. It was talking negatively to me and the angels.

"It's too late. You're too late." The evil spirit said.

I began to praise the Lord, and glorify the Lord. I was trying to remain calm and positive. I had driven for over three hours when I started to get sleepy. I could barely stay awake. I was still praying and glorifying God. We were not supposed to leave town. But if your family is in danger, you need to do the right thing. At least at the time, I thought I was doing the right thing.

At one point, I was remembering all the stuff I went through and how the Angels interfered with my life. I was getting mad at the angels that were with me. They thought they were doing me a favor, moving me to the wrong house and the wrong job. The more I thought of it the more angry I became. I was still very sleepy and then I began to cry again feeling sorry for myself. I had already driven about three hours, without stopping. I told the Angels to leave me alone. I was getting a bad feeling, just then like I needed to stop. There was a fast food restaurant up ahead. I washed my face and took a walk around the parking lot. I took some deep breaths and got back in the van.

"Forgive me angels. I'm so sorry. I'm just tired. It's all my fault. Don't leave me. God forgive me." I cried.

A few moments later, Paul told me had I not stopped when I did. I would have ran into a Big rig truck. Hitting the truck from behind and dying instantly. And because I was mad at God's Angels, I would not have been saved. Where I died, is where I was going to spend eternity as a spirit.

"A witch would have taken your spirit and hung it like an ornament on a tree among other spirits there. I would have had to search for Christian in the supernatural, to pray for you my lady. A Christian who is familiar with the spirit world, is the only way to have released you from the witch. It might have taken years to find one." Paul said.

There are many paths a person can take. From what I am told by the Angel. It is best to walk with God. To think that I almost lost my soul just because I was mad at God's Angels. This really shocked me. I was less than fifteen minutes away from my son's town. I decided to stop and call my son to see if everything was all right. He sounded happy that he and his friend were getting ready to watch a movie. I did not tell him I was minutes away.

My son was fine. So what was that all about? I thought to myself. Driving here, and thinking he was in danger. I turned the car around and headed to Santa Maria. I did not stop to see him. Something was not right. It did not feel right. Who gave me the information that he was in danger? Why did I not question who it was? Who was the source?

I was not going to see him. Something was not right. I turned the van around, and decided to take a different route home. As I was driving home, I realized I was duped. If there is such a word I was lied to. Driving gives you a lot of time to think. I was no longer sleepy. I was given bad information, it must have been from some evil spirit so that Paul and the angels would not do what the Lord wanted us to do. I felt that if we had stopped to see my son. We would have all been slain by evil spirits that were waiting for us there.

The information about my son being in danger was not from God. This would have been mistaken for disobedience. Due to the fact, we did not listen. And acted on impulse.

Which I thought was doing the right thing.

I was glad I did not see my son that evening. There were too many unanswered questions too. I have been driving more than six hours now. I was no longer sleepy but I was running out of gas. I was on an open road, somewhere near a country town. My van was full of Angels, when I stopped for gas. As I stopped the van, out of nowhere, appeared an army of evil spirits that had just arrived there. They were in the thousands. I remained very calm like if they were not there, I needed gas and to use the restroom.

Paul and the Angels stayed in the car. Good thing they did, the angels that were with me are no match for their thousands. Some evil spirits followed me to the restroom. It was a male and a female Demon spirit. There might have been others that followed. They are watching me sitting in the toilet.

"She cannot be of any threat?" The Demon female Soldier said.

"Look at her, she's just an old lady. What can she do? "She sounded like a strong military female with authority.

"We are wasting our time here." Another Demon replied. I walked out of the restroom and went to pay for gas. I heard them mock my angels.

"They have one Warrior and a couple of Angels, how sad is that." The evil spirit said.

I got in the van and drove away. We were at a distance, when Paul noticed they were following us.

"They could have killed us." Paul said.

I prayed to God for help. We were out -numbered. I was thinking of how to pray to God in this situation. I could ask God to disintegrate the demons. But how many were going to die and how many still remained. They were in the thousands. No, we needed Jesus to help us.

"Lady just keep driving." Paul said. I asked Jesus for help.

"Jesus we are outnumbered, I need you to destroy the enemy that is following us." I said. "In your name Jesus." It was only seconds when I heard.

"Jesus is coming." The Angels said.

I could not close my eyes to see it in my vision, so Paul had to describe to me what was going on. All this is happening in another dimension in the supernatural. Jesus was in spirit form, he was not here in natural . Even though Jesus is Alive now and forever.

"Jesus is coming down in a chariot." Paul said.

"Yes, in a chariot." the Angels responded. At one point, Paul got out of the car to see how many demons were following us.

"Paul, be careful" I said. "I cannot believe I told a warrior to be careful.

Jesus Warriors destroyed the Demon Warriors that were following us. "Angels described to me what was going on." I said.

"Jesus and his Angels killed the demons that were following us. The other Demons that were headed our way, retreated." The Angel said.

I thank God and Jesus for fighting a battle with the Enemy. The enemy was no match for Jesus, that's for sure. Praise the Lord. I had hoped I could have seen Jesus coming down from Heaven. I drove for more than six hours the same evening. I knew there was a rest area up ahead about thirty minutes away. I was going to stop.

When I finally arrived, I pulled out my sleeping bag and said my prayers. I do not want to be attacked while I'm sleeping. I ask God to protect me. God sent his Warrior Angels, and guarded my van while I slept.

"Thank you God, for your wonderful work this evening."

#

It was morning, when I arrived in Pismo Beach. It was very windy, walking to the end of the pier. I told the Angels to take off flying and have some fun. I was thinking of what happened last night. Driving all the way to the valley, then driving back. I reacted too quickly, without thinking things through. I asked God to forgive me. I knew we had to head back to Santa Maria. But I do not like to be in a hurry. I like to enjoy my trip unless it is a matter of life or death. I learned my lesson: don't over-react And find out who is giving you the information. God told me to do something and I did something else. Good thing, I have a forgiving God that loves me. I looked at the waves for a while.

"Angels, let's play a game. I will use my body like a clock and my arms will be like two hands of the clock. You Angels fly and shout to me where you are." I am speaking to them in my mind. The game is. "Where's the Angel?"

"Where am I?" Shouted an Angel.

Where am I? ``shouted another.

"You're at two o'clock. You are three o'clock." Speaking to them in my mind.

This went on for a while with the Angels. Not all the Angels played this game. I was getting exhausted just talking to them in my mind. I started walking back, and stopped to see a couple fishing, they looked very happy. He told her he would be right back. I smiled at the lady.

"Have you caught any fish?" I said.

"Not yet," She replied. I stood by and wondered if she was going to catch anything. It wasn't long when her boyfriend returned.

"Hello." He said.

I smiled and started walking back to the van. "Angels, did you have a good time?" I said. "Why yes, thank you. They replied.

I had hoped I could see the Angels flying about, but I know that was not possible. God has a reason for everything. I know some people can see angels like Martha, my friend.

After a couple of weeks, as I was sitting in my van looking out at the ocean waves. I was thinking of my son in Heaven and that I could speak to him. It was wonderful that God let me speak to my son in Heaven. I made a big mistake when I was young. But a wonderful thing happened, to make up for that. My son was in heaven. And I could speak to him. It felt good that I could hear him.

I close my eyes and ask God that I would like to speak to my son in Heaven in Jesus name. I believe I could, I never thought I couldn't. I don't know if I woke him, but he sounded groggy.

"Who." He said.

"This is your mother." I said. "How are you doing son?"

"Fine, I am fine. Mom please don't cry." "Okay I'll try not to. Do you have a name."

"No. How does the name Markell sound to you? It belongs to an A-mighty warrior, who is a friend of Paul and me."

"I like the name." He said.

"Good, I will call you again and use your new name. I love you son. Oh by the way, you have a grandmother in Heaven. Her name is Zenaida."

"I will call you again and use your new name son. I love you." I forgot to ask him what he does in Heaven. Another time."

I went to visit my sister's house one evening. I greeted her outside her apartment and walked in her house. I put my bag down and sat on the couch. She walked to her bedroom to put her stuff away, she had just gotten home from work. While I was sitting in the living room, I was thinking of mom. It was hard not to with all the pictures my sister has in the house.

I thought I talked to Mom to hear her voice and to see how she is doing. I prayed to God to let me speak to my mother who is a citizen of Heaven.

"A Ma," This is the name I have always called her. "Yolie"

Mom was happy to hear from me. She came down from heaven. I could hear her in the room. When I felt my mothers presence here. She asked me about everyone. I started with the oldest to the youngest of my siblings. She was interested in all their lives as I spoke to her through my mind. For some reason I can hear Heaven citizens very clearly. Mom told me to tell the family she was fine and that she loved us.

I told her I might not be able to tell them that. "They may not believe me." "How are you able to hear me?" she said Speaking in Spanish.

"I believe I can A ma." I said in Spanish.

By this time my sister walked in the living room talking about her day. I did not know where Mom was at when she walked in.

"Rachel won't hear me." Mom speaks in Spanish." "No Ma."

My sister Rachel was in the kitchen cooking now. She had turned on the television screen but I was really not watching it. Even though I was staring at it. After a short while I did not hear from my mother anymore. We ate dinner and talked about our lives and our children. I left late that evening back home.

There was another time my mother came to visit me. She had spent the whole night on Earth.

"A ma what are you doing here?" I said in Spanish

She said she wanted to stay a little longer. I told her it was not a good idea. I called Paul the Angel to take her back home to Heaven.

"Paulie, mom came to visit but did not leave." "She came last night." Senora, you can not stay here. Paul speaking to mom.

"I was a little shocked that she was here all night. Evil spirits could have hurt her." I said Goodbye to mom. And that I will speak to her another time. If the Lord permits.

When I wrote this I asked the Lord if we are allowed to talk to citizens of Heaven he said they are not allowed but he does make an exception. Paul flew her back to Heaven.

I have spoken to mom in Heaven and have sent her flowers to her quarters. I am sure it's a mansion.

#

GOD

I answered an ad for a room to rent. I told the lady I would be there at three o'clock the next day. It was not going to be on the coast. But it was not too far from the coast. I drove to Bakersfield as planned. I like the town right away, it has parks and every corner or so it seems. This time, I ask God for the right place to live. I drove to the house and said a little prayer. I saw a lady outside in the front lawn watering her garden. I drove around and parked the van across the street.

Before I even knocked at the front door I asked Paul to ask God if this is the place that God wants me to move to. I heard God speaking to Paul the angel. God was loud and clear and I was in a little shock that I could hear God so clearly. God's voice was a little like Pauls but different. It is deep, strong and beautiful and yet pleasant like his Angels. The voice was the Lord's voice. I was still in awe, that I heard God speaking to Paul the Angel, about me. Then again, Paul is one of God's angels.

"She needs a place to live and this is a good place for her." God speaking to Paul.

"She would rather live near the coast." Paul replied. I like the way Paul was speaking to God, kind of like old friends.

"She will stay at this place." The Lord said. "Yes Syer." Paul replied.

Seeing that I could hear them. I said. "Thank you God." I got my answer. This was the place for me, at least for now. Other places I moved to, I did not consult the Lord and it didn't work out. I knocked in front of the door. It was the same lady watering her plants that answered the door. She seems like a nice lady.

"Mrs. Smith? I'm the lady that wants to rent your room." "Yes, come on in."

We walked into the kitchen, there were pictures of Jesus everywhere I knew this was a place for me. We have the same interests. This is the kind of atmosphere I needed, a Christian home.

"It is going to work out just fine, I have a good feeling about you." She said,

The room was very nicely decorated and furnished. A television and internet included in the price. It was ready to move in. I really needed a place to stay. I was tired of the road. I just wanted to rest. I gave her the money for the room and moved in right away. I did not have much to move. I have only clothes and pictures that I painted.

She had two other tenants living there, including her husband. They were both in their golden years. I kept to myself and did not tell her about my Angels. There were Spirits in her house just like every place else, no different. Like I said, Spirits are everywhere.

They move into the homes. I prayed for my residence, then for the town where I was now going to be living. There will be no evil spirits here.

God will see to it. Angels came and went to Heaven, day and night. I always have Angels in my home. They live in Heaven and stay with me sometimes. And that is just wonderful, I love it. I unpacked and made it my home. Praise the Lord.

There are evenings when I take this winding road home. I do not like the fact that it's a winding road. It goes up to the mountain then does all these loops around the mountain. Then it gets worse, you almost feel like you are going to fall off the mountain. It is very dangerous.

I keep my eyes on the road. It will take about thirty minutes to get through it. I was about to turn on the radio, coming down to a mountain nearing a group of trees. I thought I heard voices outside. I rolled down the window, to hear.

"Release us." " Releases us." "Releases us." They cried.

Almost sounding like a sorrowful sad song. These are the spirits that did not make it to Heaven. They're not evil, just lost souls. Witches capture the spirits and will not release them once they are captured by them. The spirits that were crying out, were hanging on around the trees like ornaments.

"We are going to pray for the spirits that are held against their will. But only for the good spirits." I said.

The Angels and I prayed to the All-mighty God. That God would release the spirits that were hanging on the trees, if it be God's will. We praise God for his work and then ask God to tie and bind the witches that held the spirits captive. In Jesus name. As we drove along the mountain, we were praising God. Then the dead spirits were praising God. I could hear them glorifying God.

"Glory to God in the highest. Glory to God in the highest. Hallelujah, Hallelujah, Praise the Lord thank you Jesus." The dead spirits said. Praising God in a song.

This is what I heard driving alongside the mountain. We left that area with a good feeling. I don't know if I should help dead spirits, but if God did not answer my prayer then I 'd know. I continued my drive home.

I asked Angel Ron about California. He said it was headed for Earthquakes. It sadden me, because all my family lives in California

It was getting late in the evening, as I drove home from work, around nine thirty maybe closer to ten. It was still hot and humid at night, so I opened the windows to the van again. I have been on the road for a long time and was sleepy and I needed to stretch my legs. Just then, I heard an unknown angel in my van, talking to the angels that were with me. The unknown Angel flew in my van.

"Why are you here?" The Angels asked.

"She is falling asleep." The unknown Angel replied.

"No, she will be just fine. It is not her time. She has something to do for the Lord." Paul said.

Just then, I realized who the unknown Angel was. It was the Angel of Death. I turned on the radio, to wake up and begin to sing. It helped for a short time. I was not scared, just felt a little uneasy about it. I have heard and seen in my vision so many things that Death Angel did not scare me. I turn up the radio to keep me awake. The death angel left.

It wasn't long when I started to feel sleepy again. This time, the angels saw the angel of death flying outside the passenger window.

"He's coming back." Paulie. The Angel said.

The angel of death flew in the van through the window. I do not like that angel in my van, I knew he was here for me.

"It's not her time." Paul said. "You must leave. Paul demanded.

"You have no authority here." The angel of death replied.

I had heard enough, I was going to stop at the next gas station. The only problem is, it was not for another twenty minutes. I turned the radio on again, I found a station that was playing music with no foul language or nasty in it. I prayed to God to keep me awake, so I started to sing again on the road. Finally, it said Gorman exit. I could not wait for the rest area. I did not want to die. And I surely did not like that Death Angel in my van.

I drove in and used the restroom. Splashed some water on my face then went outside to pump some gas in the van. The angel of death was gone and I was fully alert..

I thought about the angel of death in my van, as I started to drive away. I could have died. It did not make me afraid though I probably should have. I did not fear the angel of death. I have had other experiences after that. There was another time, when I was driving late in the evening and feeling sleepy, a dark smoke came upon the street near my front window. It was as though it was announcing it was coming. And then there was another time, I was taking shower. I heard the angels around me.

"What are you doing here?" The Angels said.

I focused on what I heard and knew what might happen. I knew the bathtub in the shower had no mat and sometimes got slippery. I began to pray to God in the shower, that I would not die. And for God's to protect me.

I heard many angels around in the shower. I could hear what was going on in the spirit world. I am not afraid of dying, because I know where I'm going and that's to be with the Lord in heaven. But for right now, I have something to do for God. The death angel will have to wait. I'm not ready to die only when the All-mighty God says it's time.

It was going to take forty-five minutes to get home. There was another rest stop area up ahead. I felt fine and alert, for now. It depends on how I feel. I thank God for keeping me awake. I made it to the next rest area. I never walk in alone to use the restroom. I always wait for a group of women to walk in with. I got home safe that night. Lucky for me, God and his Angels are with me. Thank you Jesus

#

TOMMY

I spent a good portion of my summer at the beach. It was something I always wanted to do for a long time. If I was not at the beach, I was at community centers, libraries and I even went for a drive to Los Angeles just to stand at Azusa Street. Where God did lots of Miracles in the year 1906.

I was out late at the beach. I tried not to stay out late or especially let it get dark on me. Paul does not like me to stay out late. He told me once that the spirits come out of the ocean, late at night.

"The Dead come out at night, looking for their family." Paul said.

It normally does not bother me but I don't like the dead around either. I can sense things around me and hear spirits. I don't stay out late. The last thing I want to deal with is spirits looking for their loved ones. it's not so much that spirits bother me, it's the evil ones coming out of the sea. I already battle everyday in the spirit world.

Evil spirits try to attack me in my sleep. Sometimes by sending serpents to hurt me. That's the time, I ask for help. God sends his Warriors down from heaven and kills the serpent and sends that serpent back to Hell. God has always answered my prayers. God has always been there to fight my battles. I am very thankful to the Lord.

It was late in the evening when I drove to the grocery store. I was a little hungry. I wanted some fruit to go with my meal. It must have been about nine p.m. when I walked back to my car, that's when I heard it. The howling was not from an animal. It was an eerie sound coming from a human. I was told a human just passed away nearby..

"Noo….Noo… How could this be." The Spirit sounded like a loud howl.

The spirit was walking the Earth among the living. He had come to realize he was not in Heaven. The howling was of sorrow. They are the ones that know they are dead. And now are in the spirit world. The spirits are lied to by evil spirits known as Demons. They tell them they are Elite, Special people. Because the dead can see the living , and living cannot see them.

The spirits believe they are Elite. They do not know they are dead. They are the unbelievers. They are the ones that did not accept Jesus Christ as their personal Lord and savior when they were alive. They walk among the living. I hear this in the spirit world.

I drove away from the area. I did not want the newly dead near me. For some reason they are drawn to me. I don't know if it is because I can hear them or because I am close to God.

One evening, I was lying on my bed thinking about the Angels with my eyes closed. Paul was in the room and said he was flying back to Heaven. I have followed Paul's voice up to heaven. I could hear Paul talking to the Angels or even God in heaven at times. God's voice is beautiful, deep and heavenly. I do not know how I can hear them. But if I can, so can anyone if they believe in God and Jesus.

I was awakened in the middle of the night. My heart is beating rapidly. I know something's wrong. Either, I am under attack or one of my angels is in trouble. I began to pray to the Lord all mighty God, you say ask and you shall receive. I am asking in Jesus' name. I prayed for whoever needs this prayer, whether it be the Angels or myself, for God to please help them and heal them. Angels sometimes are in battle so whenever my heart races like that I just start praying for them or myself. I have asked Jesus to keep my family safe through my ordeal of everyday battles with the Enemy. I know Jesus Is keeping my family safe.

I recently found out I have a Guardian Angel. His name is Tommy. It has never occurred to me that I had one. I have been so busy in the supernatural world that it never crossed my mind. I asked Tommy questions in hopes he could give me answers. Sometimes he would ask Paul or Heaven above. My guardian Angel has been quiet for many years. He said he thinks of me as his daughter. He has been with me since birth. I asked him why he never spoke to me before.

" You didn't know I was with you," he replied.

I remember the first time I realized I had a guardian angel.

" Guardian Angel? Guardian Angel?" He did not answer when I called out to him.

" I did not think you were speaking to me." I thought you were speaking to other Angels nearby." The Guardian Angel said.

"I thought you would never speak to me." He said.

I talk to my Guardian Angel on a daily basis, well almost daily basis. Mostly to get a hold of Paul for me. Tommy is faster at it. He doesn't go through prayers like me. He just calls out to Heaven and finds him. It is very interesting how Tommy does that. Tommy is not that old, he is about five hundred years old. He says he is more in his teens. Tommy is like a close relative or more like my best friend, very well respected. I was told that everyone has their own Guardian Angel.

There was a time, I couldn't get a hold of Paul. I pray to God to speak to Paul, that I may hear him. Paul did not answer, on the third call. I ask my Guardian Angel to help me get a hold of him.

"Tommy, call up to heaven and find Paul for me" I said.

"Paul. "Paul." Tommy called out to Paul.. "Where are you?"

There was no answer, I know something has happened to him, he is injured or held captive by the enemy or worse. I pulled out my Bible and began praying for Paul. For God to return Paul to us. The angels pray for him too. I asked God to place Paul's body on the bed, I do not like his body placed on the floor. Then I ask for the Holy Spirit to shield around him, while he is healing. I asked God to heal his Angel body and return his Angel Spirit back to his Angel body, in the name of Jesus. God answered my prayer. God returned Paul back.

"I never used to get hurt this much before." Paul said. The enemy was trying to get to me, by killing Paul. At least that is what I'm told.

"How are you feeling?" I asked.

"Fine, my lady. What happened? I remember walking outside to talk to some guys, that's all I remember. I could not see anything, just darkness." Paul said.

"I think you have been gone for a day or so." I said. "I don't know."

"There were feathers laying all over the ground and were unrecognizable." The Guardian Angel Tommy said.

Paul then flew to Heaven. I thank God for returning Paul to us. He has never been attacked this much before that he could recall. He was gone for a couple of days. One evening, I was looking at the internet in my room, when I heard a cry.

"Help me." It sounded like an Angel.

Sometimes my angels do get hurt. I have heard them under attack. I do not know, when they get hurt, it must be, when I am asleep. Sometimes it takes me months to find out that they've been injured.

"How many angels are missing?" I asked. "Too many of us." The Angels replied.

"Let us pray for the Angels that were attacked. "That God shields the Angel with your Holy Spirit and heals the Angels. In Jesus name." I said. I always ask in Jesus' name. Jesus is the Son of God. Jesus died on the cross, which arose on the third day. Is seated at the right hand of the father. Jesus is alive yesterday, today and forever. Jesus is alive.

After that, Jesus was seen by five hundred people at once. (1 Corinthians 15 v 6)

That very same evening, I was sitting on my bed talking to the angels. That I realize, there might be a lot of Angels missing, not just months ago but years ago. I needed to pray for all of God's Angels.

"Let's pray to the All mighty-God, for the missing Angels."

We prayed for all the missing Angels going back five years. We will ask for their return. I asked God to clear the streets and place the Holy Spirit around the area, so that the angels will be placed on the streets, if the lawn gets full of Angels. I wasn't sure if I could go back that many years or if God would answer my prayer. I did not know if I could even ask God. I figured if God does not answer my prayer request, it is not because I do not believe. It is because it is not the right prayer request.

The Angels received the same prayer that was said to Paul. There are times I have been in a hurry and have said the prayer wrong. I asked God to correct my prayer when that happens. This time I knew what to say. After my prayer request to God in Jesus name. I could see in my vision. The lawn and in the street, was full of Angels that had gone missing in the past.

There were so many Angels on the street that night. This is what I saw. Praise the Lord. I asked the Angels that were with me, to talk to the Angels on the lawn and on the street. The Angels went outside to talk to them and they all praised the Lord. I had hoped I could have seen the streets full of angels that night, in the natural world. And not just in my vision. The Angels glorified God.

"Glory to God in the highest, glory to God in the highest, hallelujah hallelujah. Praise Lord." The Angels shouting and worshiping the Lord.

The praising went on for a while, then they all flew away. It was a very holy scene in my vision. It has been three years since I have been talking to the Angels. I have learned a lot from God and his Angels. I've recently been asking my Guardian Angel questions. If he does not have the answer. He calls on Paul for help. Then Paul will ask God, if I am allowed to know the answers to the question.

#

The angels and I were driving 101 freeway headed north to Santa Maria. We were heading back home. It was early winter and late in the evening, not too cold out. I was going to try a new road that was much closer. I began to sing a christian song from the radio. I asked the Angels to join in and sing with me. They were flying and following the van. We were all singing out loud to the lord. At the end of the song, one of the Angels shouted. "Glory to God". After a while the Angels came in the van because it was getting very late. We drove for a while looking for the new road to take.

"Look there is one of us." The angel said. "He is up there."

"There." Another replied. The Angel was flying alongside us. He must have noticed the van full of angels. Just then, there was a knock on the window.

"Hello there. May I come in?" He said.

"Yes you may. Only if you are one of God's Angels." He flew in and sat in the back seat with the other Angels.

"Where are you going?" I asked. "Can she hear us.? He said. "Nice to meet you."

"How do you do that?"

"You mean, because I can hear you. I just believe I can, but then, I've been seeking God for many years and reading his word. I believe I can." I said. He went to sit in the back with the Angels. As we drove towards Santa Maria.

"So where are you going?" I said.

"Well, there is a young woman that I like to visit. She doesn't know I exist. How do I get her to hear me?" He said.

"The word of God and faith." "You know she may never hear you." I said.

He talked to the Angels for a while, but as we got closer to an exit he said he had to leave. The Angel of Santa Maria flew out the window. He seemed very anxious to be somewhere. It was getting dark and late at night. I turned to the road I was looking for. I had never taken this route before and did not like the one-lane road. There were hardly any drivers on the road for a long time.

The Angels and I finally got home after driving a couple hours. It was nice running into the angel. I kind of knew that I'd get home safe after all, I only have a handful of angels with me, I thought to myself. I went straight to bed and fell asleep after my prayers, of course.

It is early spring, I got up in the middle of the night and went to use the restroom. As I was using the toilet, I could feel the bad presence here. This was an enormous serpent. I walked back to my room, I asked God to send a warrior to destroy the Demon. It was not an ordinary demon, more like a big serpent. I asked God to tie-in, bind the enemy. And for God to kill the serpent.

The Demons in the street corner, must have sent the evil spirit. They have been giving me trouble, ever since I have been able to hear the spirit world. I am sure of that. There was an evening, I was sitting there watching television with the Angels, in my room.

When Paul said.

"I have to go, my lady, "I have an urgent matter to attend."

I did not see any harm in following Paul through my mind, and in my vision. I followed him up to heaven, he picked up this flaming sword. The sword is only used when it is a very bad demon or serpent. I then followed him to his destination. There was already a Warrior fighting the Demon, a huge serpent. Markell the warrior was already fighting. He swung his sword from side-to-side, thrusting his sword at the Beast.

"Glad you could make it." Markell said.

Paul did not answer... But went into action. I could see Paul in my mind in a vision. Thrusting his sword at the enemy, he flew to the top of the Beast. He swung it to the right then to the left. Paul appeared to be trying to get a good position to kill the Beast. The Beast had quick moves too. It was a big serpent, from what I could see. The serpent was dark, ugly and enormous and looked about sixty feet tall.

The Angels are nine feet tall, and seem small next to the beast. I could feel Paul moving as he positioned himself to kill the Beast. He was awesome to see in my mind. Paul went to the right then to the top and thrusted the Beast. Then the warrior Markell went to the left side, then to the middle of the Beast. They were magnificent. In my vision

"Paul, you're wonderful." I said.

"Paul, did you leave the window open?" Markell asked

"I guess I did." Paul replied. "My lady."

"I just had to follow you." I said. Paul was not happy that I followed him, that I could sense.

"You could have gotten hurt." He said. In a deep voice. We must have flown across the sea because of his deep voice.

"How." I said.

"Because your spirit was with me," He said. "I'm sorry, I didn't know..."

I had thought I could envision him. But instead my spirit left with him. He said, I was on his wing holding on. This is what I understood, is that Paul left the window open. So I followed him to his destinations. After the battle, we left the place. I really do not know where the killing of the serpent took place, and he was not going to tell me. We flew home. He was never mad. Angels do not get mad, that's good. He took me home. I guess I wanted to witness a battle. Paul was so victorious and galient to watch. I did not realize I could have been hurt, just for traveling with him in my spirit. I was back home, and wanted to tell someone. But would anyone believe me?

#

THE CROWN

I was up all night at a lady's house. I was assigned to work there. She was not doing well. It must have been about three in the morning. When I checked up on her again.

"How are you doing?" I said.

"Fine." She said, with a smile. She was staring at me for a while. "Can you do me a favor?" She said,

"Can you take off your crown?" She said, "Crown?"... "What a crown." I said..

She then went back to sleep after a few minutes. I did not know what she was talking about. I was not wearing anything on my hair. I thought I'd get my answers from Paul. I asked God to speak to Paul.

"Paul. Paulie, this is me. I have to ask you a question." I said. "What is it my lady?"

"I'm here with this lady. She asked me a strange question. She said that I have a crown on my head. She is sincere, not crazy. She's just old. Paulie, what is she talking about?"

"God placed a crown of Saints on your head." Paul said. "What?"

"Yes, a couple of days ago, God placed a crown of saints on your head." Paul said.

I was overcome with emotion, for the Lord to have put a crown of Saints on my head. It was just the best thing that could have ever happened to me. I was stunned, I never thought I would receive such an honor from the All-mighty God. I love you God. I said. I thank God for this wonderful honor I received. The rest of the morning could not be any better. I felt so blessed. The crown of saints, I thought to myself. I just sat there on the big easy chair next to the bed. God placed a crown on my head. How Glorious was that. I thought. Still filled with amazement. I sat there for a while stunned. Later on in the day,

I thought I would ask Paul about the crown. After the initial shock was over. "Paulie... So how tall is my crown? I said.

"Two feet tall." Paul replied. "Describe it to me."

"It's taller in the front, with a ruby in the middle and different kinds of jewels all around." He said. "It's sort of pointed on top in the front of a crown, and it has a big X where the jewels meet."

"It sounds beautiful." I said. I went to look in the mirror to see it. I was not able to. "You will in time." He said. "Some people can see it."

I knew Spirits could see it. And that created a problem for me. They tried to take the crown. The spirits tried by cutting off my head then my scalp a couple of times.

The Spirits do not realize that God is not going to permit spirits to own the Saints Crown. They tried a couple of times. But God took it back from them. And placed the back of my head and healed me. The spirits and evil spirits are just about the same when it comes to crowns made of gold and jewels. I asked God not to let the Spirits see the crown on my head or feel it. It is better that way. I do not like Spirits cutting me anymore for it. Only God's Angels and Christian people can see the crown of saints that believe Jesus is alive, today and forever.

God has his reasons why I am not permitted to see the crown. I know it's in my head. I hope someday, God will let me see the Angels too. I know some people can see Angels.

#

JESUS VISITS

The year was March 2017 it was late at night, I could not sleep. I was looking at some of my paintings in the room. I noticed they were not finished and wanted to touch them up. I called Paul to come down from heaven. I wanted his company. I took the Jesus painting down from the shelf. I wanted to finish the paint of Jesus, the one Paul has mistaken for Jesus. I have been touching up my oil paintings for years. I was painting Jesus' eye color when he arrived. It was Jesus.

"Sire." Paul said. There were two or three angels in the room with me that evening. Jesus came into my room and was talking to Paul and his Angels. I really did not know what to say to Jesus the son of God, except.

"I hope it's a good likeness of you." I said.

"It's fine." Jesus said. I wanted to see my portrait." I was honored to have Jesus' presence in my room. I did not know how to address Jesus. I got a little nervous while I was painting. Jesus was in my room...Jesus was in my room. I kept repeating. He never manifested to me.

"Should I call him your Holiness?" I thought to myself. Knowing full well that they could hear my thoughts.

"Thank you. Your Holiness." I said. Jesus was still talking to the angels that were with me. After a few minutes, Jesus left my room. I was still amazed and speechless, I did not know what to say. I guess with everything that has happened to me. I have learned to remain calm.

It was now, about four in the morning. I needed to get some sleep. I was still thinking about Jesus. I cleaned my brushes and went to bed. I wanted to call my best friend and tell her about Jesus visiting me. But I did not want to boast about it. And would she believe me? Better wait, I thought.

One evening, I was sitting on my bed. My heart started racing, as it did when my angels were in trouble or I was in danger. I began to pray for us. Thanking God for always answering my prayers. I tried to get a hold of Paul. Paul was not answering me, after several attempts. Feeling a little nervous. I asked my Guardian Angel. Please help me find Paul.

"Hey Paul, where are you?" The Guardian Tommy asked. "Paul, where are you?" I asked.

"My lady, I do not know where I am?" I'm in deep space somewhere, "Where in space are you?"

"I am not sure? Maybe, several galaxies away." Paul said. The angels and I prayed for Paul.

"God show Paul your Angel a guiding light, to follow back home." " He is lost in space." " I pray that you almighty God the creator of Heaven and Earth." " You are the Alpha the Omega." "The beginning and the end." "The God of Abraham, Isaac, Jacob and Moses." "Please return Paul to us. in Jesus name." In my vision, I could see Paul following a beautiful string of lights back to heaven. It looks like waving swirling bright beads. Paul returned to us. I gave him a hug, even though I could not see him.

"Paul what happened?" I said.

"I was on a mission, when I got hit by a meteor storm." "I must have been unconscious for some time." Paul said. "I tried to find my way back." "I guess getting hit on the head, I lost my sense of direction" Until I heard your guardian angel calling out to me." I then saw a string of lights and followed them." Thanks for praying for me." Paul returned back to Heaven that evening.

One weekend, I took a drive to the beach, and made other stops, to pick up food, I put gas in the car. By the time I arrived at the beach I was feeling tired. I park my car in a secluded area of the beach, facing the water. I reclined the seat of my car and I fell asleep. When I woke up, I was startled. I thought I went off the road. I pulled the seat up so fast, not realizing an Angel was on my shoulder. That he flew off my shoulder out the car onto a rock. I could not see him as you know, But could sense he was hurt.

"It's Paulie, he is hurt badly." The Angel said.. I kept calm and prayed for him. I didn't know if he was dead or alive. I asked God to heal him and restore his Spirit back to his Angel body, in Jesus name. I felt bad that he got hurt, even though God healed him.

Angels are very nice, thay do not get mad and are very forgiving.

We stayed at the beach for a while and watched the waves. Paul and the Angels flew around the beach and I just walked the shoreline. I looked out there and hoped I could see them flying. I could hear them talking to each other as they were flying. I spoke to the Lord, how beautiful he made the world. And for everything he has shown me.

The next day I drove to the park in Santa Paula. I pulled out my paintings of Jesus and the Angels. I was alway retouching the paintings. I had already finished painting another portrait of an Angel. I then pulled the painting Jesus. I was painting for a while out there in the middle of the park. When I heard his voice, it was coming from Heaven. It was God.

"My son is lighter than that,"God said. I was caught by surprise. To hear God's voice from Heaven. I was afraid to look up at the sky. Eventually I did.

"I will do my best." I said. I will remember this for a long time. The day I heard the Lord speak to me, from Heaven. At that time, I only heard God's Angels. And of course, the time I heard the Lord speaking to Paul about me. This time, God spoke to me. I did not hear anything more than that. I wanted to say more but was afraid. Which makes me wonder. Why did I not speak to God? After a few hours of painting, I went home.

I was returning from my hometown. It was about nine pm or so. I was returning home from visiting my relatives there. I still had about an hour on the road and I was getting really sleepy. I put on some music to keep me awake, it only helped for a short time. I then prayed to God to keep me awake.

"God please do not let me fall asleep on the road." I said. Just as I finished my prayer. Jesus' presence was in my van and he was sitting in the front seat. I did not pull off the road. I kept on driving.

"Jesus I am so glad you are here." I said. "I don't like what happens when I get sleepy." I did not see Jesus, but I do know it was him.

"How are things? I said. I was lost for words, again. Here was Jesus in my front seat and still I did not know what questions to ask him or how to greet him. I drove for some time before. Jesus asked me a question. Jesus' voice was so soft and pleasant. He had a message for one of my children. It was for Steve.

"Steve and his family need to start attending church." Jesus said. I was nearing my street, where I rented a room at this house. I turned the corner, it was a quiet night. And thank Jesus for spending time with me, keeping me awake on the drive home.

"I will give him the information." I said. I got out of my van when Jesus left. It was about two in the morning as I was walking down the street toward the house. I felt very good about speaking to the Lord. I thought the enemy could not be nearby. Because Jesus was just here.

I walked into the house, I did the same thing every day before I entered the room. And that is to pray to God, to rebuke the spirits that are in the house and in my room. I got ready for bed. I thank God for a good day for always answering my prayers and that he would protect me as I slept through the night.

#

I have been thinking of asking God to take me out of Spirit World. But will I still hear Angels.? I hope so. I am afraid of not hearing the Almighty God's Angels. I do get tired, always being on guard. The fight with the enemy will always go on now. It tries to do horrible things to me in my spirit. I can hear them from hundreds of miles away, before they even get near me to attack. But I must remember it's God's fight. I pray for the Lord to fight my battles. I only survived because I believe in Jesus and that he heals me when I ask. My spirit can not die in the supernatural world, my flesh cannot survive without my spirit. I have learned that Jesus took all these sins when he died on the cross and arose in three days. That we that believe in him might be saved and healed. It is our right according to the scriptures. Jesus won the battle over 2000 years ago.

I have heard this before but it took some time to truly understand the meaning of it. Jesus took our sickness, our disease, every bad thing in our life and took it to the cross. We have the right, the authority to ask God to be healed from all disease or whatever bad thing we are going through. Because Jesus took all that for us. Yes, that is what I believe and that is why we, I have the authority to ask Jesus in his name to take all that away.

Lately I have been speaking to the Holy Ghost, more often than my Guardian Angel. I find that the Holy Ghost gives me the answers more quickly. I consulted the Spirit of the Lord in writing notations throughout this book. I have stopped helping the dead spirits out of trees. The spirit of the lord told me not to be helping them anymore.

My Guardian Angel is awesome, he is doing a good job. Though he is not a warrior. He does have some skills. At times my Guardian angel Tommy has had to fight some battles too. Tommy is more like family. He says he has been with me since birth. And when I could not find my Guardian Angel. I asked God to heal him and return him back to me. He is a very brave Angel and knows how dear my Guardian Angel is to me. He also has been through alot in my travels.

I want to thank God and his Angels that have traveled with me. I have had the pleasure of hearing and speaking with God and his Angels, even though the Angels are not permitted to manifest to me. Thank you God for being with me and supporting me with their positive presence and ability to handle every situation.

For God's warriors they are wonderful; they go right into battle to protect me. I thank God for entrusting me with his Angels and the new Angels with me. It is a pleasure to know them and others to meet their acquaintances. It is an honor and pleasure to have traveled with God's Angels. I praise you Almighty God.

I wrote what I heard and saw in my visions in the Supernatural World. I want to thank God again for letting me hear the Supernatural

World. And the visions he gave me to see what was going on in the supernatural. And for all the wonderful dreams about things I needed to know. And for the warning he placed in my heart, to let me know when I was in danger in the supernatural world. Thank you Almighty God for healing me and your Angels. Through the name of your Son Jesus. And for bringing back all your Angels that had gone missing.

Thanks to Jesus, I can not thank you enough. For fighting the enemy, when we were being chased. And visiting us, all those times, some I did not mention in the book. I know you live now and forever. Matthew 20:19

I thank the Holy Spirit. For being right there in the middle of the battles. And Shielding me from the enemy, when I asked. And for helping me write this book. I want to thank Paul, the Angel. He has been a lot of help to me in my travels and adventures in the supernatural. He has not manifested to me yet, but I hope someday he will. It has been more than three years now, I am still learning the Word of God. God, Jesus and the Holy Spirit are the Trinity of God.

God told me to write this book. By sending his messengers to tell me. And then, about a month ago, God reminded me of the book. God called my Book.

"My Biography."

I left out some stories that happened to me, per God's request. All these stories in this book happen to me in the Natural and the Supernatural World. I feel truly blessed, hearing God's voice and his Angels. And the pleasure to have traveled with his Angels.

Written by   YOLANDA MONTALVO

Put on the whole armor of God, that you may be able to stand against the wiles of the devil. For we wrestle not against flesh and blood, but against principalities, against the powers, against the rulers of the darkness of this world, against spiritual wickedness in high places. Ephesians chapter 6:11 chapter 6:12.